Bagatelle

EXECUTIVE DIRECTOR
Suzanne Tise-Isoré
Style & Design Collection

EDITORIAL ADVISER
Karine Huguenaud

EDITORIAL COORDINATION
Lara Lo Calzo

EDITORIAL ASSISTANT
Cécile Baribaud

GRAPHIC DESIGN
Clément Prats

TYPESETTING
Joseph Tsai

TRANSLATED FROM THE FRENCH BY
Deke Dusinberre

COPY EDITING AND PROOFREADING
Lindsay Porter

PRODUCTION
Élodie Conjat

COLOR SEPARATION
Les Artisans du Regard, Paris

PRINTED BY
Verona Libri, Italy

Simultaneously published in French as *Bagatelle. Une folie à Paris.*

Éditions Flammarion
82, rue Saint-Lazare
75009 Paris
editions.flammarion.com
@styleanddesignflammarion
@flammarioninternational

23 24 25 3 2 1
ISBN: 978-2-08-024752-0
Legal Deposit: 09/2023

Nicolas Cattelain

Bagatelle

A Princely Residence in Paris

Flammarion

Contents

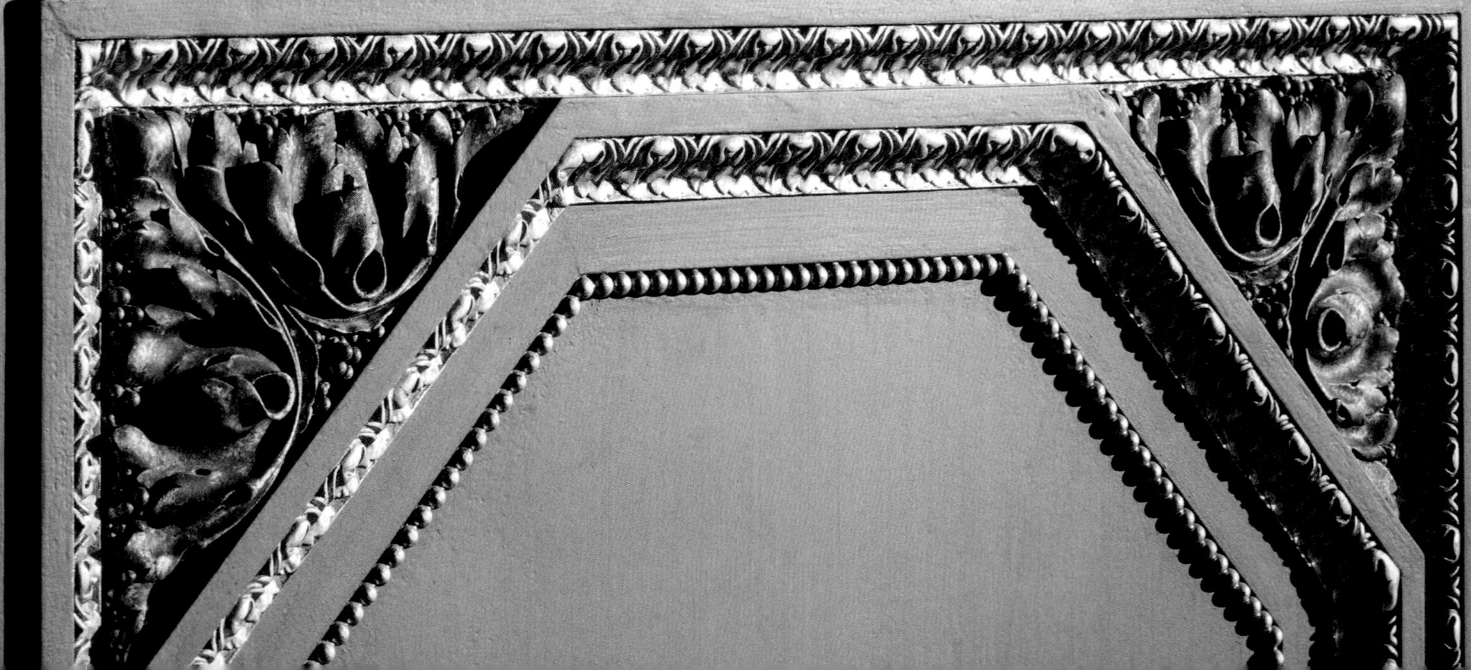

Foreword

"There were places much grander and richer, but there was no such complete work of art, nothing that would appeal so to those who were really informed."

Henry James, *The Spoils of Poynton*, 1897

The Bagatelle pavilion has long embodied, for me, eighteenth-century French taste: an exquisite place with perfect proportions whose extreme refinement extends to tiny details such as the gilt-bronze mounts on the fireplaces by Marie Antoinette's favorite bronzesmith, Pierre Gouthière. The pavilion nestled in the Bois de Boulogne, a wood halfway between Paris and the château de Versailles. Thus removed from court etiquette, Bagatelle was an archetypal "pleasure house," the eighteenth-century term for an inhabitable little folly built by aristocrats and rich financiers in the environs of Paris, often on a whim and in a very short time, defying considerations of time and money. Bagatelle was built in sixty-four days in 1777 as a wager between the comte d'Artois (Louis XVI's younger brother) and his sister-in-law, Queen Marie Antoinette, both being scarcely twenty years of age. As a place of fun and forbidden treats, of entertainment and frivolity, Bagatelle was a cure for the era's ill: boredom. My knowledge of Bagatelle was limited to one of the few histories of the place, *La Folie d'Artois* (1988), which dealt primarily with the eighteenth century. And my professional career, notably research into Pierre Gouthière, led me to focus on the pavilion solely during the days of the comte d'Artois.

One of the qualities of this book by Nicolas Cattelain is that it tells the story of Bagatelle from the very beginning up to the present. The author begins this history in the early eighteenth century, when a certain Lucie Félicité de Noailles owned a little home—also called Bagatelle—on the spot of the count's future pleasure house. Cattelain fills in and sometimes corrects details of the ups and downs of the premises in the days of the comte d'Artois, but above all he continues the tale into the nineteenth and twentieth centuries. Cattelain informs us—to my own great surprise—that the count's "folly" was not only a paean to eighteenth-century France but that it also incarnated the nineteenth century through a series of famous owners. Following the comte d'Artois, Napoleon I and Empress Marie-Louise briefly occupied the pavilion (where their young son, styled the King of Rome, would play), before becoming the property of the duc and duchesse de Berry, where it served as a cradle for another royal prince, the duc de Bordeaux. In 1835, Bagatelle was bought by the marquess of Hertford, who bequeathed it to

PAGE 5
Nestling in the Bois de Boulogne near Paris, the pavilion called Bagatelle is the eighteenth-century archetype of an exquisite little home built for its owner's personal pleasure.

FACING PAGE
Detail of the main entrance door to Bagatelle.

Sir Richard Wallace in 1870, after which it was purchased by the City of Paris in 1905. Again to my great surprise, this little neoclassical building turns out to be not a perfect embodiment of the Louis-XVI style but rather a challenge to the history of French art and tastes. Right from the start, Bagatelle's architecture was surprising in terms of plan and façade, having been inspired by Palladian-revival villas discovered by the English architect William Chambers during a trip to Italy around 1750. Yet it was not surprising, according to Cattelain, that the pavilion's architect, François-Joseph Bélanger, had never been to Italy (unlike most artists and architects of his generation), since he traveled regularly to England, where he saw the neoclassical works of Chambers and Robert Adams. The irony, as stressed by the author, was that the "English" quality sought by Bélanger and the young comte d'Artois—the most Anglophile prince at the French court—was effaced in the 1860s by an Englishman, the rich collector Lord Hertford, who decided to make Bagatelle more "French" by giving it a façade of proportions typical of the Louis-XVI style of 1770–80. That was when the role of the pavilion also changed; conceived in the eighteenth century as a pleasure house where people rarely spent the night, it thereafter became a regular residence for Hertford and his illegitimate son, Sir Richard Wallace.

This book's originality also resides in its fascinating tale of the characters who lived in Bagatelle. We thus discover not only the complexity but also its private side, in which wives, mistresses, friends, advisers, and gardeners play an often crucial role. We come to realize that, through its history, Bagatelle attracted characters who resembled one another: they were close to the powers that be (by chance or by force, not necessarily legitimate); were enthusiastic connoisseurs (people "who were really informed," in the words of Henry James quoted in the epigraph); were lovers of history, curious about life and somewhat offbeat for their times. Bagatelle seems to have served above all as a haven for its occupants.

Obviously, it is hard to know the aspirations, ambitions, dreams, and desires—not to mention fears—of those who built, renovated, and lived at Bagatelle. It is equally hard to know if they loved the place, if their time there was happy. Yet that is the challenge taken up by Cattelain in this book: he offers a different take on the history of an aristocratic residence that became a palace for art collectors. In so doing, he naturally relies on early studies of Bagatelle, as well as the many biographies of its illustrious residents. Yet he also gleaned valuable information from much more academic sources, as well as a few discoveries in France's national archives. Cattelain's real contribution, however, is his scrutiny of a great quantity of memoirs, correspondence, and other types of journal penned in the eighteenth and nineteenth centuries by English as well as French writers; these materials constitute precious sources of information directly from people who visited or lived at Bagatelle over the centuries yet had heretofore escaped historians of the comte d'Artois's little pavilion. Cattelain's account is dotted with many anecdotes and quotations, allowing us to really see the private side of Bagatelle. Readers will discover that this book is not an accumulation of information gathered over time by Cattelain and those who preceded him, but is the history of a place such as it was known and experienced by its contemporaries. Finally, I must praise the choice, quality, and quantity of illustrations, old and recent, that impart life to a text that is as pleasant to read as it is learned.

This book is being published at a pivotal moment in Bagatelle's history, coinciding with a new renovation of the pavilion, its outbuildings, and the Trianon erected by Lord Hertford around 1870. In 2020 the City of Paris assigned management of the Bagatelle estate to the Fondation Mansart, headed by Albéric de Montgolfier. Renovation of Bagatelle was jointly

FACING PAGE
Detail of a snake-shaped latch on an upstairs window at Bagatelle.

VUE DU PAVILLON DE BAGATELLE
du côté de l'entrée,
Construit en 64 jours sur les dessins d'Alexandre Belanger premier Architecte de Mgr. Comte d'Artois

overseen by Montgolfier and Cattelain—the foundation's treasurer—assisted in their decision-making by an advisory committee composed of eminent specialists of the field: Daniel Alcouffe, former head of the Louvre's Department of Decorative Arts; Christian Baulez, former executive curator at the château de Versailles; Xavier Bray, director of the Wallace Collection in London; Jean-Jacques Gauthier, former inspector of the Mobilier National; Christophe Leribault, director of the Musée d'Orsay, and myself. Renovation work was awarded to architects Perrot & Richard, known for their restoration and protection of major monuments of French heritage.

While the historic and cultural importance of Bagatelle made restoration a priority, there is the question of *how* to restore the pavilion, what future role it should play. This book naturally provides a roadmap. According to a well-known, well-practiced rule of the renovation of historic buildings, it is imperative to preserve the last reliably known state—in this case, mainly the exterior architecture and interior decoration of the days of Lord Hertford. There is, however, one major exception, namely the music room, whose eighteenth-century state has miraculously survived, and can thus testify once more to the lavishness of the days of the comte d'Artois. In the other ground-floor rooms—the dining room, billiard room, entrance hall, boudoir, and the count's old bathroom—the woodwork dates largely from the eighteenth century, but in the nineteenth century was entirely repainted in "Versailles gray" heightened with gold; the polychrome ceilings of the count's day were lost and replaced by imitation skies; all the fireplaces were changed. These rooms, as renovated by Lord Hertford, can therefore express the taste of a nineteenth-century English art collector who loved eighteenth-century France, through a selection of furniture, decorative art, paintings, and sculptures. They can be arranged in a profusion typical of the Second Empire (1852–70), as seen in photographs of Bagatelle taken by Charles Marville around 1860. Upstairs, the comte d'Artois's private apartments—comprising five bedrooms, three antechambers, and two private compartments—still survives, but the rooms were thoroughly altered by Hertford when he decided, around 1860, to raise the ceilings. The rooms thus lost their original ceilings and the upper part of the woodwork—the cornice area—was changed. (Meanwhile, the famous gilt-bronze mounts made by Gouthière for the comte d'Artois's fireplaces were stolen in the 1980s.) These relatively small rooms (between 100 and 150 square feet) could therefore evoke the history of Bagatelle's various owners through the decorative objects, furnishings, manuscripts, prints, and paintings that belonged to them, with a preference for those items that were actually kept at Bagatelle. In this pursuit, the Fondation Mansart started to make major purchases thanks to dynamic patronage. Worth stressing is the purchase of a watercolor, done in 1777 by Jean-Démosthène Dugourc, of the comte d'Artois with Bagatelle in the background, as well as the acquisition of an armchair for the bathroom and a suite of salon furniture (three armchairs and six chairs) made for Bagatelle by Georges Jacob, cabinetmaker to the king, around 1780.

Once the restoration has been completed, Albéric de Montgolfier wants to bring Bagatelle back to life as described in these pages by Nicolas Cattelain: a place where everyone can fall in love with art, architecture, and gardens, or simply enjoy a walk among its beautiful grounds. Following in the footsteps of the comte d'Artois, the duchesse de Berry, the marquess of Hertford, and Sir Richard Wallace, the new caretakers of the premises will weave links with history while devising exhibitions and events that should make Bagatelle a key venue of cultural life in Paris.

Charlotte Vignon

FACING PAGE
A few of the books essential to any study of the history of Bagatelle, notably an album of engravings of "picturesque views of France" and Chateaubriand's memoirs regarding the life and death of the duc de Berry (collection of the author).

Introduction

To my children

"Bagatelle! Could any better name illustrate more clearly this little architectural gem that can now be visited by the public? Its life has hardly been long—what is two centuries in the span of history? Yet in that brief period, what vicissitudes has this dwelling witnessed, what adventures—romantic and tragic—has it harbored!"

Charles Gailly de Taurines, *Aventuriers et femmes de Qualité*, 1907

"To live over people's lives is nothing unless we live over their perceptions, live over the growth, the change, the varying intensity of the same—since it was by these things they themselves lived."

Henry James, *William Wetmore Story and His Friends*, 1903

PARVA SED APTA

The history of France might be a vast novel, twelve thick volumes sturdily bound in leather, with dozens of chapters and long paragraphs describing, in small print, important events and leading figures. But it might also be a series of short stories in which we glimpse stealthier goings-on, the everyday lives of tragic heroes: their joys, hopes, misfortunes, successes, and failures, indeed their youthful years and their later regrets. These stories would show us châteaus, parties, gardens—the finest settings devised by the greatest artists, whether now demolished by the heartless or rescued by the visionary. In them we would find artworks that were admired, looted, and lost, only to be recovered and loved anew. They would recount the ambitions, passions, tragedies, and follies that constitute the grand—and the petty—history of France.

The saga of Bagatelle is one of those stories. It began in the early eighteenth century. We glimpse the regent enjoying the pleasures of life, Mademoiselle de Charolais teaching Louis XV the ways of the world, and Marie Antoinette making a crazy wager with her brother-in-law, the comte d'Artois; we see a Palladian residence being built in just sixty-four days yet becoming an inspiration for the greatest architects, with landscaped grounds that would later be lauded by Marcel Proust. We watch Napoleon as he dreams of a timeless empire, Joséphine as she weeps at the feet of a child-king, the duchesse de Berry holding a "miracle baby" in her arms, and an imperial prince taking riding lessons. Finally, in this same house and same grounds of Bagatelle, we admire one of the finest collections of art ever assembled, thanks to an English peer and his illegitimate son, both great lovers of French art. Two centuries of private lives, two hundred years of historic events—all at the gates of Paris.

People have always been fascinated by Bagatelle's rich history. Back in 1909 Henri Gaston Duchesne published a major book on it, and in the late twentieth century there appeared two scholarly works that remain authoritative: *La Folie d'Artois* (1988) and *Bagatelle dans ses Jardins* (1997). To my great advantage, the literature has grown since then. Without citing all the new sources, it is worth mentioning Charles-Éloi Vial's PhD dissertation on imperial and royal hunts in the early nineteenth century, as well as more recent publications on eighteenth-century architecture, notably by Alexia Lebeurre and Claire Olagnier, new biographies by Évelyne Lever and Laure Hillerin, plus many studies on the history of art collecting in the eighteenth and nineteenth centuries, for example Suzanne Higgott's book on Richard Wallace.

Much of my work of documentation and writing was done during the months of lockdwon. Online research tools and remote access to the sites of major book stores were a great aid. Each week brought its share of overlooked memoirs, publications from an earlier era, sometimes obscure studies, and nineteenth-century magazines and catalogs, which in turn were full of surprises, discoveries, and new trails that enlivened my days of isolation. I would like to thank all the connoisseurs, memoirists, booksellers, scholars, and authors of yesteryear and today for the enlightenment and pleasure they gave me.

The reader will thus understand that writing this book was an immensely satisfying task for me, and I am now delighted to be able to share it with all of you. Very many people contributed to the effort. I would first of all like to thank Albéric and Audrey de Montgolfier, without whom the Bagatelle renovation project would never have gotten off the ground. I am also grateful to Alexis Robin and everyone at the Fondation Mansart, Matthieu Gillet and the Perrot & Richard architectural firm, and finally, Antoine Courtois and all the teams at Ateliers de France, who are

PAGE 13
The courtyard façade of Bagatelle. The entire exterior of the château—façades, roofing, and wood and metallic finishings—were restored in 2021 and 2022 thanks to the patronage of the Fondation Mansart.

FACING PAGE
Detail of floral grotesques painted on the inner shutter of a window. A major campaign to restore the eighteenth-century interior of the music room is planned.

devoting so much time and energy to the Bagatelle renovation. A special thanks to Jacques Garcia for his exceptional help in this renovation project and for having been at the genesis of this book. I am equally grateful to all the patrons who contributed to the restoration of the château, without whom it would have been simply impossible.

With regard to this book itself, I would like to thank Charlotte Vignon above all. Her many pertinent suggestions, her commitment, and her generosity and patient editing were for me a particularly precious aid and encouragement. My gratitude also extends to other members of Bagatelle's advisory committee—Daniel Alcouffe, Christian Baulez, Xavier Bray, Jean-Jacques Gautier, and Christophe Leribault—as well as all those people who contributed to this publication in one way or another, sharing their sources, access, comments, or sometimes simply their great ideas. In no particular order, I would like to thank Sébastien Évain, Mathieu Caron, for his invaluable research, Danielle Kisluk-Grosheide, Meredith Martin, Suzanne Higgott, Helen Jacobsen, Mia Jackson, Marie-Hélène Didier, Yves Carlier, Anne Forray-Carlier, Bénédicte Gady, Carole Blumenfeld, William Iselin, Alexandre Pradère, Étienne Bréton, Hervé Aaron, Éric Coatalem, Bertrand Gautier, Bertrand Talabardon, Ary Jan, Alexis and Nicolas Kugel, Marella Rossi, Benjamin Steinitz, Christian Prévost-Marcilhacy, François-Joseph Graf, Mario Tavella, Simon de Monicault, Isabelle Bresset, Thierry Maudret, and Christophe Parant. I also owe a special debt to Susan Weber, whose example served as a daily inspiration.

This book would obviously have never seen the light of day without the determination and backing of Suzanne Tise-Isoré and her entire team at Flammarion, notably Karine Huguenaud.

My warm thanks also go to Lionel and Ariane Sauvage, Philippe Champy, President of the Fondation La Marck, as well as to Max Blumberg and Edouardo dos Santos Araujo for their remarkable support for the Bagatelle renovation and book—and for their friendship.

Finally, I'd like to take the opportunity to pay tribute to all those people who have helped me in the past, allowing me to be where I am today, publishing my first book. There are too many names to list—they know who they are. Yet I would simply like to mention Henry Kravis and George Roberts, without whom nothing would have been possible, and who have my deepest gratitude.

Nicolas Cattelain

FACING PAGE
Detail of one of the two sphinxes wearing the nemes, or pharaonic headcloth, on the terrace overlooking the main courtyard. The original sculptures, in Conflans stone, were subcontracted by Nicolas François Daniel Lhuillier to Philippe Laurent Roland; they now stand on the terrace opposite the Trianon.

PAGES 18–19
The château de Bagatelle seen from the terrace that now overlooks the road leading from Sèvres to Neuilly. Renovation work in 2022 restored the delicate hues of the "simple yet noble" architecture of this French-style pavilion.

PARVA SED APTA

Chapter 1

Bagatelle before Bagatelle

Behind the Scenes of Royal Intrigue

"Mademoiselle [X] speaks wonders of Bagatelle, we both wish to be there. It is no mere bagatelle for us, your trifles are well worth others' substance. Is it far from Paris? For even though you always manage to get the most out of things, I hold that good company must remain within striking distance of the capital. In the long run, pleasant society is life's greatest delight, and it can be found only in capital cities."

Letter from Philip Dormer Stanhope,
4th Earl of Chesterfield, to Mademoiselle de Charolais, July 31, 1747

Le Mont VALERIEN. Autrement dit-
Le Calvaire. 2 lieues de Paris.
15. la vigne de Mad.lle Coulon
16. la vigne de Mr. de la porte
17. maison de Mr. le duc de Marmotier
18. mais. de Mr. de Ste Marie
19. la porte du port
20. le passage du barc
21. le batteau de Surenne
22. l'abbaye de loncham
23. la vigne de Mr. Mazot
24. platriere de Mr. Richer
25. la Riuiere de Seine.
Seine
Riuiere
Loncham

The Bois de Boulogne, a wooded park on the outskirts of Paris, became a favored place of social interaction among French elites by the late seventeenth century. A history of Bagatelle must therefore begin with the history of the Bois.

A former oak forest and hunting ground for French kings from Dagobert onward, the Bois de Boulogne was particularly appreciated by Francis I, who built the château de Madrid there in the early sixteenth century. By the early eighteenth century, the Bois also became a place for promenades and country retreats. Indeed, the abbey of Longchamp, located in the woods, became a new meeting place for Parisian high society, which came to hear a celebrated soprano, Mademoiselle Laure, who sang services at the request of the abbess.

> It was soon whispered in Paris that in order to hear [Mademoiselle Laure], you had to attend service at Longchamp. Hence when Holy Week arrived, a throng of carriages could be seen along the path through the woods to the abbey; and everyone said they were enchanted by this promenade through the countryside.... The stream of France's leading families to the abbey's services, the resulting atmosphere of sociability and elegance, and the participation of onlookers all contributed to make an outing to Longchamp a crucial event in the history of French habits and Paris luxury in the eighteenth century.[1]

The Longchamp abbey and the new role played by the Bois de Boulogne in Paris social life were the subject of many accounts, including the following:

> April 1774: Mademoiselle Dervieux is at Longchamp, where every fashionable Parisian woman must retire during Lent. The word "retire" suggests some pious isolation ... but eighteenth-century society has long since adapted all religious events to its pleasure. The abbey of Longchamp has become a fixed-price abode of retreat open to young sinners as well as repentant old ladies.
>
> After the services on Holy Thursday and Good Friday, the colorful crowd strolls along the tree-lined lane ... women compare their charms, their attire, and their lovers; coachmen rival one another, their teams bedecked with flounces. People go to Longchamp the way the curious go to the Salons—many to look, a few to buy. A woman whose delightful company was judged to be a mere one hundred louis the previous year will double in value, or even rise to a thousand.[2]

In this context of social effervescence, the country house known as Bagatelle already enjoyed a certain rank in court life and was often mentioned by the great memoir writers of the day, such as the marquis d'Argenson, the duc de Luynes, and the bourgeois chronicler Edmond Jean Francois Barbier. Courtiers went there in search of fun or to hatch a plot. One king after another took his guests—and his mistresses—there.

Louis XV—Louis XIV's great-grandson—was only five when he ascended to the throne. Louis XIV's nephew, the forty-one-year-old Philippe II d'Orléans, was named regent. First the regent, then the young king, would take advantage of the pleasures offered at Bagatelle. They were welcomed there by the maréchale d'Estrées, herself a neighbor and close friend of Mademoiselle de Charolais—known simply as "Mademoiselle"—who lived in the outbuildings of the château de Madrid.

PAGE 21
Imitation Gothic ruins, erected on the grounds of Bagatelle in the nineteenth century by Joseph-Antoine Froelicher, architect to the duchesse de Berry, evoke the abbey of Longchamp (after which they are now named). The abbey itself, where Parisian high society gathered in the eighteenth century to flirt in the surrounding woods, was demolished in 1794.

FACING PAGE
A colored print, made around 1660, shows Mount Valérien and, in the foreground, the abbey of Longchamp. A fort built on the hill from 1841 to 1846 bombarded Paris during the Prussian occupation in 1870, then during the Commune in 1871, damaging some of Bagatelle's outbuildings.

PAGE 25
Pierre-Denis Martin, *View of the Château de Madrid*, oil on canvas, 1723 (Châteaux de Versailles et de Trianon, Versailles). The château de Madrid was home to Mademoiselle de Charolais, who colluded with the maréchale d'Estrées to use Bagatelle for encounters that would advance her own position at the royal court.

"The party on the trip to La Muette currently taken by the King [Louis XV] is merry and independent. They have invited the ladies who usually take part and to whom one is accustomed. They dine at [the château de] Madrid with Mademoiselle [de Charolais], they sup at La Muette; in the afternoon, at Bagatelle, home of the maréchale d'Estrées, they pass the time gleefully, making love, if you please."

Journal et mémoires du marquis d'Argenson,
April 17, 1739

"Mademoiselle" was Louise-Anne de Bourbon Condé, great-granddaughter of le Grand Condé. Rejecting all offers of marriage, she preferred to live a "free" life in the château de Madrid but continued to play a political role through her influence over the private life of the young Louis XV. Mademoiselle liked to have her portrait painted wearing brown Franciscan robes, which gave rise to all kinds of rumors and inspired Voltaire to write satirical verse about her.

The "maréchale"—or field-marshal's wife—was Lucie Félicité de Noailles, married to Victor Marie d'Estrées, a duke as well as a marshal, from an illustrious aristocratic family. The marshal bought Bagatelle in 1720 but rarely enjoyed the premises, devoted as he was to his career and to his collection of books and objets d'art in his Paris mansion on rue de l'Université. His wife lived at Bagatelle. The childless, ambitious maréchale incarnated the dissolute morals associated with the Régence period. With her friend Mademoiselle, she turned Bagatelle into a pivotal focus of intrigues at court. What did Bagatelle look like at the time? The duc de Luynes left a description:

> The house is very small. On entering, to the right is a fairly large drawing room, but filled by a table that seats twenty. To the left is an antechamber that is used as a dining room and can hold a table for twelve to fourteen. Further on is another drawing room, then a bedroom. Above and in the attic are seven or eight comfortable lodgings; the house overlooks the walls enclosing the Bois de Boulogne.... The courtyard is paved, and can hold five or six carriages; to right and left are two flowerbeds, to which are added, over by the woods, groves divided by little clearings that vary the promenades.[3]

A drawing by architect François-Joseph Bélanger of "the former house of Bagatelle" shows no fewer than fourteen windows on the façade. The house, then, was not all that small. Yet it had neither the scale of a château with everything such a building implies, nor the diminutiveness of a thatched hut. It was an imposing country home: practical, designed to host guests, with a garden laid out for delightful strolls. In his diary, Barbier described a party given by the maréchale d'Estrées in honor of the regent in August 1721. On that occasion the duc d'Orléans was fêting his new mistress, Madame d'Averne, who had replaced Madame de Parabère.

> Tuesday, 12th: The maréchale d'Estrées organized a supper for the regent and Madame d'Averne in her little house on the edge of the Bois de Boulogne, opposite the water and the house of Monsieur de Hurche. Her house, although called Bagatelle ["trifle"], cost at least one hundred thousand livres. That same day I supped in a nearby house in the woods, and we saw everyone pass. I admired the boldness of the regent, who knows—or should know—that people have no cause to love him, and who was nevertheless in a carriage with the maréchale next to him and Madame d'Averne in front, with only two footmen, no pages or guards.... They boated on the water prior to supper; we heard, from over the terrace, the musical festivities.[4]

There was at the time a dense network of residences, royal or otherwise, around Paris and Versailles—including Bagatelle, Madrid, La Muette, Saint-Germain, and Saint-Cloud—where one could reign or, on the contrary, simply enjoy oneself or withdraw from the din of the world. Mademoiselle de Charolais and the maréchale d'Estrées fully grasped how to use such residences to their advantage. When Louis XV assumed full powers in 1723, the two women

FACING PAGE
Attributed to Jean-Baptiste Van Loo, *Louis XV Dressed as a Pilgrim of Saint James*, oil on canvas, c. 1725 (Châteaux de Versailles et de Trianon, Versailles). Seated beneath a term with the head of Pan, the young king wears the sash of the Order of the Holy Spirit across his chest and holds a staff and a gourd—attributes of pilgrims of Saint James of Compostela. It was at Bagatelle, with the complicity of Mademoiselle de Charolais, that Louis XV met several of his alleged mistresses.

PAGES 28–29
Eugène Lami, *A Supper with the Regent*, watercolor and gouache, 1854 (Wallace Collection, London). The dissolute behavior during the Regency found a home at Bagatelle, where the maréchale d'Estrées received the regent, Philippe d'Orléans. This watercolor by Lami was bought by the nineteenth-century owner of Bagatelle, Lord Hertford, shortly before he died in 1870.

"Angelic friar Charolais,
tell us how it came to pass
that monkish rope, in such array,
doth serve as girdle to our Venus."

Voltaire, "Impromptu à Mademoiselle de Charolais"

were well entrenched—and ambition went to their heads. The marquis d'Argenson recounted what might be called the "Mailly conspiracy" in September 1738:

> His Majesty's mistress, Madame de Mailly,[5] was often obliged to go to the home of Mademoiselle de Charolais ... because from there it was convenient for her to go spend the night at La Muette when the king was there.... From that requirement arose Mademoiselle's familiarity with His Majesty, but soon that favor turned into ambition. Mademoiselle ... in collusion with her lover, the bishop of Rennes, and the maréchale d'Estrées ... proposed to sell the maréchale d'Estrées's house in the Bois de Boulogne, called Bagatelle, to Madame de Mailly, which would have placed said mistress under the close supervision of the obliging Mademoiselle. The plan did not come off.[6]

Argenson castigated such excessive ambition in florid language: "This triumvirate would thereby govern the kingdom through the king's mistress. Ambition wormed into their heads, this is how woman was tempted by the serpent." Once the plot stalled, Madame d'Estrées sided with the winning party. "Abbe V, a friend of H, was of great use; having made up with the maréchale d'Estrées, he learned all their secrets and dissuaded her from this risky scheme, for she might soon lose her much-needed support from the king."[7]

Mademoiselle and the maréchale d'Estrées thus lost that battle, but not the war. "Till the day she died, the maréchale and her faithful *Mademoiselle* were a power within government, like ministers in petticoats. More than ever, the Court, the king, and his favorite took the discreet path to the little house in the woods where pleasure parties followed one another."[8]

The habit seemed ingrained, and royal visits continued (as did the merry-go-round of mistresses) when Mademoiselle's good friend, Madame de Monconseil, became the new occupant of the premises around 1746–48. Ten years after the failure of the Mailly scheme, Argenson noted once again on September 30, 1748, "This is a serious matter. The king is in love with the princesse de Robecq, daughter of M. de Luxembourg.... It is claimed that on his latest trip to La Muette he went on a stroll to Bagatelle, that the princesse de Robecq was there, and that the king and the lady vanished for a quarter of an hour."[9] That could be considered no less than a coup d'état against the king's official mistress, Madame de Pompadour:

> The princesse de Robecq was delightfully pretty, high-born, a Montmorency, daughter of the maréchal de Luxembourg who, the wags would claim, took a lively interest in the king's flirtations. Very recently married, she was practically a child, with a simpering air so mocked by Voltaire. She had everything required to arouse the King's somewhat blasé whimsies. Recently, therefore, all of Madame de Pompadour's numerous enemies turned with a curiosity full of hope toward the pretty little princess's pleasing if irregular features.... The visit to Bagatelle, which gave life to these hidden hopes, immediately sparked veiled but persistent musings: "A quarter of an hour, a quarter of an hour!"
>
> Alas, the quarter hour at Bagatelle had no sequel at Versailles. Madame de Pompadour was too solidly anchored to the king's heart to allow her to be so easily banished; her "reign" would last another fifteen years, and poor Madame de Robecq—disappointing illusion, swiftly vanishing mirage—had to content herself with those fifteen minutes of favor.[10]

PAGE 31
Charles-Joseph Natoire, *Portrait of Louise-Anne de Bourbon Condé, called Mademoiselle de Charolais*, oil on canvas, c. 1740–60 (Châteaux de Versailles et de Trianon, Versailles). Great-granddaughter of Le Grand Condé, Mademoiselle de Charolais led an unbridled life in the château de Madrid; she liked to have herself painted as a penitent, dressed in Franciscan robes, as here. Along with her friend Lucie Félicité de Noailles, she turned Bagatelle into a center of court intrigue.

FACING PAGE
Jacques Rigaud, *View of the Château Royal de Madrid on the Promenade from Paris in the Bois de Boulogne*, etching, c. 1730 (collection of the author).

With Madame de Monconseil, Louis XV seemed to be following the same path blazed by the maréchale d'Estrées. But history would decide otherwise. The new mistress of the house only briefly benefited from royal visits. The growing ascendency of Madame de Pompadour and the relative decline, then death, of Mademoiselle ultimately led the king away from Bagatelle. He went instead to the residence called Parc-aux-Cerfs, in what is now the Saint-Louis neighborhood of Versailles.

The party wasn't over, however. Madame de Monconseil's lively manner and her penchant for entertainment were too well suited to the temperament of the house. Fun was to be had. But the court had changed, and so had the entertainment—the real theater now took center stage.

Thanks to the marquise de Prie, then all-powerful mistress of the duc de Bourbon, Madame de Monconseil had been placed, as soon as she was married, as a lady-in-waiting in the queen of Poland's household. That privilege lasted just one year, but King Stanislaw felt benevolent affection and even true friendship for Madame de Monconseil. When Stanislaw went to Versailles to visit his daughter—who had become queen of France upon marrying Louis XV—the former lady-in-waiting made every effort to convince him to stop at Bagatelle, an opportunity to organize new festivities and performances and restore Bagatelle's past luster. "Madame de Monconseil, who was lady-in-waiting to the late queen of Poland, and toward whom the king of Poland showed much kindness and friendship, is giving, in a little house in the Bois de Boulogne, called Bagatelle, formerly owned by the maréchale d'Éstrées, a dinner for the king of Poland on the day he leaves, and this dinner is to be followed by a little party."[11]

In that way Madame de Monconseil could keep up with other aristocratic country homes near Paris, where hosts showed great imagination when welcoming friends to festive spectacles that were both simple and "bucolic," yet carefully orchestrated. Accounts of her parties were carefully transcribed, documenting the art of this domestic theater.[12] The authors were professional writers, but the performances mingled actors with hosts and guests in often comic situations. The transcription notably describes the visit of the king of Poland on September 29, 1756, and the show performed on that occasion, just a few weeks after other festivities had been held in honor of the duc de Richelieu. "His Majesty arrived at Bagatelle, and was seated at table as soon as he got down from the carriage; time was short and the quaint entertainment had to take place during the dinner, with all the verses that went with it."

In his memoirs, the duc de Luynes described another of these fêtes, enlivened by the presence of Madame de Monconseil's little daughter, nicknamed "Bijou," along with her cousin. "Two little girls aged ten or so—one of whom is Madame de Monconseil's daughter and the other her niece, Mademoiselle de Blaye—advanced toward the king and each paid him a compliment in verse. Little Monconseil then presented him with the flowers she was holding. A troupe thereupon arrived...." These players performed a little "harangue," followed by a dinner that was "most large, most refined, and most pleasant in appearance." The gathering then moved to the garden for the main attraction: "At the end of the lane was a kind of small room, surrounded by frames of glass and covered by cloth on which was written, 'Au Grand Café de Bagatelle.' In the middle of this room was an armchair facing a table on which sat a fine porcelain coffee service. The two girls mentioned above came toward the king of Poland, one handing him a cup, the other a sugar bowl. His coffee was poured and at the same time the entire company was served."[13]

FACING PAGE
Louis-René Boquet, *Mademoiselle Lionois* [*sic*], pen and ink and watercolor, 1764 (Bibliothèque Nationale de France). Boquet designed this costume for a ballerina known as Mademoiselle Lyonnois for the 1764 premiere of *Rose and Colas*, a one-act play with music by Pierre-Alexandre Monsigny. This was the very play performed by Queen Marie Antoinette on May 20, 1780, for the first party given in her honor at Bagatelle.

PAGE 36
Jacques Rigaud, *View of the Château de la Muette and Part of the Grounds*, etching, c. 1730 (collection of the author). The châteaus de Bagatelle, Madrid, and La Muette were part of a dense network of royal and private residences near Paris, becoming sites of government as well as pleasure.

"This is a serious matter. The king is in love with the princesse de Robecq, daughter of M. de Luxembourg.... It is claimed that on his latest trip to La Muette he went on a stroll to Bagatelle... that the princesse de Robecq was there, and that the king and the lady vanished for a quarter of an hour."

Journal et mémoires du marquis d'Argenson,
September 30, 1748

Attractions followed one another in each of the garden's groves. The chronicler of the *Année Littéraire* was full of praise. "Of the several festivities I have witnessed or have heard described, few seemed to me so wonderfully devised, so pleasantly executed, as the one given on Monday the 5th of this month for the King of Poland, duc de Lorraine et de Bar, by the marquise de Montconseil [*sic*] at her château of Bagatelle in the Bois de Boulogne. I am able to describe it to you, having had the honor of following His Majesty, and the pleasure of witnessing all the ingenious amusements prepared for his welcome."[14]

Delighted with the day, the king of Poland thanked his hostess most graciously. "You have chosen, dear friend, a thankless subject for all the fine compositions heard in a gathering as gallant as the one you have arranged—but not a thankless heart, for I am truly most grateful. Anything that I may ever see of such kind will seem a bagatelle when weighed against what your charming Bagatelle has yielded. Please accept my tenderest thanks, and rest assured that I shall always cherish this memory with heartfelt affection."[15]

Alas, the glamorous guest died in 1766. And the cost of maintaining Bagatelle became too high for Madame de Monconseil, despite her stipend as a former lady-in-waiting and the successful marriages of her daughters. Adélaïde—little Bijou—became a princess upon marrying Charles de Hénin-Liétard, nicknamed "prince of dwarfs" due to his stature. But the ostentatious expenditures of the Hénin couple made headlines in the newspapers and Bagatelle could not be saved.

By the late 1750s, significant repairs were already needed and Madame de Monconseil, who only had usufruct, and not title, to the property, asked the court to finance them. There followed correspondence addressed to the marquis de Marigny, then superintendent of Royal Works as well as the brother of Madame de Pompadour, but with no true results. Unable to pay for the upkeep of the dilapidated premises, she let the tenure to a Monsieur de Boisgelin on June 30, 1772. The tenure then passed through several hands until it came into those of the comte d'Artois. A letter from royal architect Jacques-Germain Soufflot to the marquis de Marigny documents the condition of the building:

> Some time ago Prince Eynen [Hénin] did me the honor of mentioning the poor condition of the house called Bagatelle, near the château de Madrid; I had the honor of replying that I had long been aware that the house was worthless, and that if one did anything to it, great expenses might entail; that Madame de Monconseil had expended money on it when she had the tenure, but without adding much to its solidity."[16]

The building was near collapse, beyond repair. The comte d'Artois would have to demolish it before rebuilding. The year was 1775. Artois was the younger brother of Louis XVI, who had been king of France for a year; and he got on particularly well with his sister-in-law, Queen Marie Antoinette. Times had changed since the Régence period and the early reign of Louis XV—and so had tastes. The time had come for a new building, a new saga. The time had come for a wager.

FACING PAGE
Martial Deny, after Fanche, *Charles Philippe of France, Comte d'Artois, Brother of the King*, c. 1780, colored print (Châteaux de Versailles et de Trianon, Versailles).

PAGES 40–41
The motto *Parva sed apta*—"Small but suitable"—refers to the modest size of the building erected for the comte d'Artois. Taken from a poem by Horace, the motto was first affixed to the Pages' Pavilion, then moved in the nineteenth century to the château, just below the sculpted frieze originally on the façade. The frieze features a medallion with Medusa head flanked by two winged sphinxes and acanthus leaves.

PARVA

SED APTA

Chapter 2

Genealogy of a Country Retreat

The Folly of a Count's Wager with a Queen

"[F]or three weeks the Queen [Marie Antoinette] has been overly indulging in objects of dissipations, which the Parisian public does not look upon too favorably. The comte d'Artois, who is concerned only with frivolity, often decides to hunt deer in the Bois de Boulogne. Given their proximity to Paris, these hunts draw a number of young people, men and women. After the hunt, the count hosts dinners in small country houses located in those very woods of Boulogne. Those dinners, without being absolutely indecent, are nevertheless much too gay."

Letter from Mercy-Argenteau to Maria Theresa, May 18, 1775

The construction of the château de Bagatelle in 1777 was intimately linked to a notorious bet between Marie Antoinette and her young brother-in-law, the comte d'Artois, as mentioned in the collective memoirs begun by Louis Petit de Bachaumont, dated October 22 of that year:

> In the Bois de Boulogne, there is a kind of weekend cottage called Bagatelle. The prince [the comte d'Artois] takes a decided interest in the trowel, and, in addition to buildings of all kinds already begun, numbering five or six, desired to enlarge and embellish this one—or, rather, to change it completely, making it worthy of himself. He adopted a tactic to finance. He wagered 100,000 francs with the Queen that this magical palace would be begun and completed during her sojourn at Fontainebleau, so that he could give a party for H[er] M[ajesty] upon her return. Eight hundred workers are there now. The count's architect truly thinks he'll win.[17]

The genesis of this wager can be traced to multiple sources: the personality of the comte d'Artois, his relationship with the queen, life at court early in the early reign of Louis XVI, and the stage set in the Bois de Boulogne.

The best clues are to be found in the correspondence between the Austrian ambassador, comte de Mercy-Argenteau, and Empress Maria Theresa, who reigned over the Holy Roman Empire and consolidated the Franco-Austrian alliance by marrying her daughter Marie Antoinette to Louis XVI. The above-quoted letter from Mercy-Argenteau, dated May 18, 1775, ends as follows: "The Queen could not resist the comte d'Artois's pressing requests that she join his hunts, which are merely promenades. Although, rightly, H. M. never remained for any of the dinners that concluded these hunts, in Paris it is seen with much regret that the Queen is associated with the revels given by the count, whose frivolity is increasingly costing him public esteem."[18]

The relationship between the queen and the count, so critical to the construction of Bagatelle, was the subject of constant complaints addressed to Marie Antoinette by Maria Theresa and her ambassador right from the moment Louis XVI was crowned king in May 1774. As the empress wrote to her daughter on July 16, 1774, "The comte d'Artois is said to be excessively bold. It is not appropriate for you to tolerate him, for in the long run it may hurt you badly. One must keep one's place, play one's role."[19]

Marie Antoinette replied on November 16, 1774. "True, the comte d'Artois is turbulent and does not always maintain the correct bearing, but be assured, dear Mother, that I know how to stop him when he begins his questionable behavior; and far from allowing familiarity, I have more than once given him mortifying scoldings in the presence of his brothers and sisters."[20]

Mercy-Argenteau wrote a second letter to Maria Theresa, on May 18, 1775:

> I cannot fail to mention once again the Queen's liaison with the comte d'Artois. This liaison, although somewhat altered, is still too frequent and overly familiar. The hunts are continuing in the Bois de Boulogne, and the young prince's frequent silliness, the King's rather unfavorable opinion of him, and the censure that his behavior arouses in the public, all increase the risk that the Queen will be compromised by the ribaldry of her brother-in-law the prince.[21]

PAGE 43
The porch of the rotunda on the garden side. The sphinxes with putti on their backs replace the sculptures that had been there until the late nineteenth century.

FACING PAGE
Queen Marie Antoinette accompanied the comte d'Artois and the comte and comtesse de Provence to a costume ball during the carnival of 1785. This print, based on costume designs by Louis-René Boquet and published in the *Magasin Pittoresque* in 1843, evokes the queen's friendship with her brother-in-law, a relationship criticized by her mother, Archduchess Maria Theresa of Austria, who feared that Marie Antoinette's reputation would be damaged.

ABOVE
A chair of white-painted beech wood, made by Georges Jacob, bearing Bagatelle's branded mark. It is one of six bought by the Fondation Mansart thanks to the patronage of the Fondation La Marck. Jacob was one of the main suppliers of furniture for Bagatelle.

FACING PAGE
After Antoine-François Callet, *Charles Philippe of France, Comte d'Artois*, oil on canvas, 1779–80 (Châteaux de Versailles et de Trianon, Versailles, on indefinite loan to the château de Compiègne). On the young prince's French-style jacket are arrayed the grand emblem and blue sash of the Order of the Holy Spirit, the insignia of the Golden Fleece, and the cross of the Order of Saint Louis.

Maria Theresa to Marie Antoinette, June 2, 1775:

> I admit that I was pained to see in the printed papers that you are indulging more than ever in all kinds of outings with the comte d'Artois in the Bois de Boulogne at the gates of Paris, without the King being present. You know better than I that this prince is held in very low esteem, and that you are thus sharing his faults. He is so young, so thoughtless; that might yet pass for a prince, but these faults are rather too great for a queen who is older and who was held in much higher esteem.[22]

Marie Antoinette replied to her mother on June 22, 1775. "I am annoyed that my dear mother judges my outings in the Bois de Boulogne on the basis of public papers. They are often wrong, and always exaggerate. The day that I was with the comte d'Artois, the king was hunting where it was absolutely impossible for me to accompany him."[23]

Marie Antoinette's protests are hardly convincing, and her relationship to Artois didn't change. For several more years, until the early 1780s, the two friends continually indulged in endless games and entertainments. The existence of this rather special relationship was linked to their personalities, to the conditions under which Louis XVI came to power, and to the stifling atmosphere at court early in the reign. It was this set of circumstances that brought the château de Bagatelle into being.

In 1775, the French royal family was composed of young adults who grew up in the courts of Europe, who married for diplomatic reasons before ever meeting their future wives and husbands, and who were largely "left to their own devices." On the death of their grandfather, Louis XV, on May 10, 1774, the three heirs in line to the Bourbon throne, Louis Auguste, duc de Berry (who became Louis XVI), Louis Stanislas Xavier, comte de Provence (who would later become Louis XVIII), and Charles Phlippe, comte d'Artois (later King Charles X), were aged, respectively, nineteen, eighteen, and sixteen. Their father, the dauphin Louis de France, had died back in 1765, and their mother, Maria Josepha of Saxony, in 1767. Meanwhile, their eldest brother, Louis Joseph Xavier, duc de Bourgogne, had died in 1761. The comte d'Artois, completely orphaned at ten, was thus the youngest of the close-knit brothers.

Memoirists and biographers of the royal children claim that their education was poor. The duc de La Vauguyon, in charge of that education, "was little concerned with Charles Philippe, who was not expected to reign; he focused his attention on the new dauphin—the duc de Berry—and on the comte de Provence, who was eager to learn. Charles Philippe showed little aptitude for study. He preferred games, jokes, and outings in the grounds of Versailles, displaying precocious social skills."[24]

Dynastic marriages did in no way compensate for the immaturity of the future kings of France. Provence and Artois married two girls from the Savoy family, namely Marie Josephine in 1771 (aged seventeen) and Maria Theresa in 1773 (also aged seventeen—the comte d'Artois had just turned sixteen). Both singularly lacked personality. A few years previously, Marie Antoinette was herself only fifteen when she married Louis Auguste, just fifteen months her elder. Meanwhile, the two surviving daughters among the siblings, Marie-Adélaïde (called Clothilde) and Élisabeth, were the youngest of all, born in 1759 and 1764.

FACING PAGE
Jean-Démosthène Dugourc, *The Comte d'Artois in Uniform with Bagatelle in the Background*, graphite, watercolor, and gouache, 1777 (Fondation Mansart, acquired thanks to the patronage of the Foundation La Marck). The twenty-year-old count is shown in front of the recently built château de Bagatelle. He poses in the uniform of a colonel-general of the Swiss and Grisons guards—red cloak with blue collar, lapels, and cuffs embroidered with silver—as his regiment maneuvers in the background.

PAGE 50
Gabriel-Jacques de Saint-Aubin, *Marie Antoinette on Horseback*, pen and ink, graphite, black chalk, and gray wash, 1777 (Musée du Louvre, Paris). The queen regularly attended hunts and horse races held by the comte d'Artois in the Bois de Boulogne.

M·L
La Reine a Cheval

"I do not believe that the comte d'Artois, in the early years of his youth and that of the Queen, was, as has been said, madly in love with his sister-in-law's beauty and kindness; indeed, I can affirm that I always saw the prince keep a highly respectful distance from the Queen, that she spoke of him and his kindness and gaiety with a casualness which accompanies only the purest feelings, and that everyone surrounding the Queen saw, in the fondness she showed for the comte d'Artois, nothing other than an affectionate sister for her youngest brother."

Mémoires de Madame Campan, c. 1775

When Louis XVI and Marie Antoinette ascended to the throne in 1774, at the head of Europe's most powerful kingdom, there was no figure of authority, no guardian to oversee the behavior of the young royal family, of which they were henceforth the eldest. True, the abbé de Vermond acted as Marie Antoinette's tutor, and the old comte de Maurepas was a close adviser to the king early in the reign, yet both were just part of the complex mechanism of court and very much involved in its intrigues. As such, they had no direct authority over the king's younger brothers. Marie Antoinette, of course, was "monitored" by Mercy-Argenteau and "guided" by the often-complaining letters she received from her mother, Maria Theresa, and her elder brother, Joseph, who paid her several visits in Paris. But that proved insufficient. Furthermore, she took two initiatives that contributed to undermine both her husband's authority and the oversight exercised by the court.[25]

First, Marie Antoinette maintained a very familiar relationship with her brothers-in-law and two sisters-in-law, for example organizing regular dinners among the three couples, sometimes with Marie-Adélaïde and Élisabeth. These gatherings sustained a particular closeness with Artois, who displayed very little deference toward his brother the king, even in public. "From that moment onward, the greatest friendship sprang up among the three young couples. They took their dinners together and only ate separately on the days when their dinners were public.... This custom, for which there was no prior example at court, was the work of Marie Antoinette, who maintained it with the greatest perseverance."[26]

Endowed with little natural authority, Louis XVI's position was further weakened by his lack of an heir. Rumors abounded at court concerning his unconsummated marriage and his reputed impotence. The royal couple's first child, Marie-Thérèse, styled Madame Royale, was only born after eight years of marriage, in 1778, while the first male heir, Louis Joseph, was born in 1781, only to die young, in 1789, during the Estates General. Meanwhile, the birth of Artois's first son—Louis Antoine—as early as 1775 destabilized both Louis XVI and his wife.

Second, Marie Antoinette sought to thwart the dominance of the two leading families at court, namely the Noailles—which included her lady-in-waiting, whom she dubbed "Madame Etiquette"—and the Rohans. Instead, she favored the Choiseul clan, and above all she brought to court Yolande Gabrielle de Polastron, comtesse—later duchesse—de Polignac, who had been her friend and confidante since 1775. The "Polignac clan" thus become the keystone of what became "the queen's party," which reinforced Marie Antoinette's friendship with her brother-in-law, and largely contributed to the deterioration of her public image right up to the Revolution. Her father, Holy Roman Emperor Francis I, had warned her in a prophetic letter that, "Friendship is one of the sweets of life, but one must be careful on whom one bestows it and not be too prodigal with it."[27] To no avail.

A key figure within the Polignac clan was the comte de Vaudreuil. Born in the Caribbean colony of Saint-Domingue in 1740, aged only twenty-four he inherited a vast fortune built on sugar plantations and the slave trade. He was both the official lover of the duchesse de Polignac and the best friend of Artois. Devoting most of his time and money to society life, Vaudreuil was the perfect companion on the countless hunts and debauched parties held by the young Charles Philippe.[28]

FACING PAGE
Niklas Lafrensen, *Festivities Held at the Petit Trianon on Monday, June 21, 1784, in Honor of King Gustav III of Sweden*, gouache on paper, 1785 (Östergötlands Museum, Linköping). Illuminations, fireworks, and surprise effects: entertainment was a true art of living at the court of Louis XVI.

"The company one keeps is a delicate matter; often it leads us, despite ourselves, toward things into which we would not have fallen without it.... Friendship is one of the sweets of life, but one must be careful on whom one bestows it and not be too prodigal with it."

Holy Roman Emperor Francis I to his children,
December 14, 1752

Everything thus conspired to throw Marie Antoinette and Artois together: the quest for fun, a penchant for games and bets, and endless entertainments. It all compensated for the young queen's isolation at court, the vexations she experienced, and her difficult relationship with her husband. On his side, Artois found a way to fill his pointless existence in a kind of headlong stampede. Left on his own, with no future prospects for a government or military career, with no one in authority to guide or restrain him—but rather, surrounded by friends and courtiers who egged him on—Artois spent money heedlessly, went slumming in Paris salons and gambling dens, and acquired mistresses from every walk of life. He would drink and gamble, wagering big and losing big. He led a life of beauty, pleasure, debauchery. Alexandre Marie Léonor de Saint-Mauris-Montbarrey (lieutenant-general of the army under Louis XVI, and named minister of war in 1778 as a protégé of Maurepas), gives this enlightening yet balanced portrait:

> Monsieur the comte d'Artois, pretty as a painting—with a truly elegant French figure and a perfectly pleasant face, bringing to mind the ideal French prince as depicted by all historians, poets, and novelists—had all the spirit and vivacity of youth, all the outer grace and gallantry that earned him the nickname *Galaor* as soon as he entered society; indeed, he boasted all the features the poet attributed to that legendary hero. This appearance and vivacity made him the prince of youth; he was always surrounded by the young people at court and was a model for the city. But while these light graces played in his favor, and while the pleasure of attracting a glance from him delighted all the young courtiers, the latter had, in exchange, filled this young prince's heart with every desire and every penchant in order to excuse everything they dared permit themselves through the lofty rank of the guide they appeared to follow.
>
> From the count's personal qualities, and from the eagerness with which all the youth at court flew to his side, we can judge how many relationships must have drawn him to the Queen's own court and induce him to take part in its pleasures and entertainments, as well as the intrigues that might arise there.[29]

Viewed from court and from Paris, Marie Antoinette's company and friendship appeared almost as an encouragement, or at least tacit approval, of the young prince's dissolute life and lavish expenditures. This reflected badly on the queen herself, considerably damaging her reputation, just as Mercy-Argenteau and Maria Theresa had anticipated. "He [the comte d'Artois] was, by his pleasant character, graces, and perhaps even his ribaldry, the littlest sibling—he did one foolish thing after another, but the king would merely scold him, forgive him, and pay his debts. Alas, the one debt the king couldn't meet was the discredit brought upon his own head and that of the queen."[30]

So much for the character of the comte d'Artois, for his lavish tastes, his uncontrolled spending, and his friendship with the queen. Was he also a man of taste, indeed, a collector or patron?

Ever since the end of the Régence period the French royal family had no longer been at the center of the French art scene.[31] Neither Louis XV nor his grandson were collectors—or even art lovers. Queen Marie Leszczynska had not shone in that sphere, Marie Antoinette still less. In addition to gambling, Marie Antoinette loved theater and music above all.

PAGE 54
Élisabeth Vigée-Lebrun, *Yolande Gabrielle Martine de Polastron, Duchesse de Polignac*, oil on canvas, 1782 (Châteaux de Versailles et de Trianon). An intimate friend of Marie Antoinette since 1775, the duchesse de Polignac was the mainstay of "the queen's party" at court, which sanctioned the queen's relationship with the comte d'Artois and thus helped to undermine her public reputation prior to the Revolution.

FACING PAGE
Jean-Baptiste Philibert Moitte, *The Comte d'Artois in Hunting Dress*, gouache, c. 1780 (Musée de Picardie, Amiens). It was in the Bois de Boulogne that the count carried out his favorite pastime, hunting, along with a new entertainment imported from England: horse racing. Bagatelle can be glimpsed behind the page holding the count's horse.

PARTIES DE
L'AMERIQUE MERIDION
et
ISLE DE S. DOMINGUE

So we have to look elsewhere for the source of inspiration and emulation that guided Artois in his early accomplishments. Two figures played a key role here: the count's long-time friend, the ubiquitous comte de Vaudreuil, and Jean-Baptiste Pierre Lebrun, the equally ubiquitous picture dealer.

Lebrun, born in 1748 and possibly descended from Charles Le Brun, was the son of painter Pierre Lebrun and began a career as an artist himself. But this was before he put down his brushes and went into the business of selling art. Keen on documentation, familiar with restoration techniques learned from his father, and a tireless traveler, by 1755 Lebrun became one of the most active picture dealers in Paris. He attended all auctions, opened his own gallery, and was known and sought out for his connoisseurship. Although he held no office at court or with the Royal Works, he became the "keeper" of the collections of both the duc de Chartres and the comte d'Artois—their private curator, in a way. Lebrun had a good eye, especially for Flemish painting, stimulating its popularity in fashionable salons. He was notably responsible for one of the most important "rediscoveries" of the age—namely that of Vermeer.[32] He also promoted contemporary artists, selling their paintings in his gallery and occasionally commissioning work.

In 1776, Lebrun married Louise Élisabeth Vigée, a young but already highly successful portraitist. That same year she painted several portraits of the comte de Provence, the sittings for which she described in her memoirs. "There were occasions when, no doubt for the sake of variety, he would sing during our sittings; not indecent songs, but songs of such a basic nature that I was baffled to think by what means such silly ditties might appear at court. Also he always sang terribly out of tune. One day he asked me, 'How do I sing, Madame Lebrun?' 'Like a prince, monsieur, I replied.'"[33]

In 1777, Vigée-Lebrun received her first commission to paint a portrait of Marie Antoinette. The Lebrun couple's salon was becoming an epicenter of the Paris art scene. The greatest artists, art lovers, collectors, and dealers gathered there for memorable evenings. Among the guests, the comte de Vaudreuil was already a client of Jean-Baptiste and would become one of the greatest art collectors of the pre-Revolutionary period. He also came to be Élisabeth's passionate lover.[34] Seventeen years older than the comte d'Artois, Vaudreuil was in many ways his guide and instructor, and the presence of paintings by Boucher, Greuze, and Fragonard in the boudoir of Bagatelle may well be a tribute to Vaudreuil's influence.

Vigée-Lebrun's memoirs stress her lover's qualities:

> Born into a high-ranking family, the comte de Vaudreuil owed more to nature than privilege, although he was singularly blessed with the latter. As well as those advantages that come from holding a powerful position in society, he possessed all the qualities, all the charm that make a man amiable: he was tall, well built, and his bearing exuded a remarkable degree of nobility and elegance; his expression was gentle and sensitive, his features as agile as his thoughts, and his engaging smile drew one to him immediately.... His favorite society was usually that of artists and the most distinguished men of letters.... He was passionately fond of all the arts, and his knowledge of painting was outstanding.[35]

FACING PAGE
François-Hubert Drouais, *The Comte de Vaudreuil*, oil on canvas, 1785 (National Gallery, London). The comte d'Artois's best friend was the comte de Vaudreuil, a member of the Polignac clan and the perfect companion for the count's pleasure-loving lifestyle. He was also known to be a connoisseur of art and a great collector of paintings.

Vigée-Lebrun went on to criticize life at court as an alienating, morally corrupting waste of time, but she followed it with a fine portrait of Vaudreuil's friendship with "his Prince:"

> Too often his position drew him away from a world to which he felt drawn by his keen mind and love of the arts; on the other hand he also found some enjoyment in his distinguished role at court, a role bestowed upon him for reasons of personal merit and for being an honest and loyal subject. Besides, he adored his Prince, Monsieur le comte d'Artois, whom he never abandoned in his misfortune, but did not flatter either. Such friendships, when one of those involved is born close to the throne, are rare indeed, and the friendship was truly mutual.[36]

In conclusion, Vigée-Lebrun quoted the comte d'Artois's reply, long after the Revolution, to a reproach by Vaudreuil, who mentioned their thirty years of friendship: "Shut up you old fool, you must be losing your memory, you've been my best friend for *forty* years."[37]

There we have the world of the comte d'Artois, Marie Antoinette, the Polignac clan, the art dealer Lebrun, and finally, Vaudreuil, the old friend, the elder, the instructor. These were the actors in a comedy of gilded youth. We need merely set the scene. Louis XIV's younger brother had no lack of options when it came to spending his money, displaying his magnificence, splurging on follies—he had properties at Versailles, the Temple, Saint-Germain, and Malmaison. So why choose Bagatelle?

As Mercy-Argenteau informs us, the count was particularly fond of the Bois de Boulogne, where he organized outings disguised as hunts and also indulged in his latest hobby—thoroughbred racing. Openly Anglophile, the comte d'Artois became enamored of this English pastime, in which the betting cost him dearly (as did playing games for stakes). Most likely, some of the "overly gay" suppers hosted by the comte d'Artois around 1775 in "small country houses located in those very woods," (Mercy-Argenteau), were held precisely in the Bagatelle premises formerly occupied by the maréchale d'Éstrées and Madame de Monconseil. Indeed, the property was then owned by Pierre d'Hénin, brother of Charles d'Hénin, who was married to Adélaïde de Monconseil and captain of the count's guards.

Artois being well acquainted with the Hénins and a frequent visitor to the Bois de Boulogne, it was only natural that he bought Bagatelle on November 1, 1775. He took his time, however, to start the works, which only began in 1777. That year, as customary, the court moved to Fontainebleau for the hunting season. Marie Antoinette chided her brother-in-law for having done nothing about the state of the Bagatelle house.[38] As Bachaumont's chronicle reported, Artois took up the challenge, wagering 100,000 francs that a new château would be entirely built before the queen returned to Versailles in six or seven weeks' time.

This wager perfectly illustrates the count's world view and its growing divergence from the course of history. The young man was the very incarnation—the last and perhaps the most brilliant—of the refined French spirit, but he also embodied all the contradictions of ancien-régime "culture" and hence the seeds of its destruction. That "culture" was one where people were not judged according to their title, profession, or accomplishments in life, but rather on the effect they made on their entourage. And that effect was the product of physical appearance, careful attire, elegance, ease and quality of conversation, and the panache with which they did

FACING PAGE
Heinrich Guttenberg, after Jean-Michel Moreau, *The Meeting in the Bois de Boulogne*, etching, between 1776 and 1779 (Musée Carnavalet – Histoire de Paris, Paris). The woods' reputation as a venue for flirtatious, indeed libertine, encounters is attested from the early eighteenth century onward.

La Rencontre au bois de Boulogne

"In addition to all that, a few days before leaving for Fontainebleau, the comte d'Artois decided to raze a little house he owns in the Bois de Boulogne, called Bagatelle, and to entirely rebuild, to new plans, a house that would be arranged and furnished in time to give a party for the Queen when the court left Choisy to return to Versailles. At first everyone thought it was absurd to attempt and complete such an undertaking in six or seven weeks. And yet this is just what was done thanks to nine hundred laborers of all kinds, who were hired to work day and night."

Letter from Mercy-Argenteau to Maria Theresa, November 19, 1777

things. From that perspective, Artois was the most perfect of refined spirits—but way out of step with a period that was increasingly concerned with monitoring royal power and controlling public spending and the raising of taxes. In this respect, Artois and history were taking two opposite paths. One is rarely forgiven for getting history wrong.

Whatever the case, the die was cast. Mercy-Argenteau described the outcome of the notorious wager:

> In addition to all that, a few days before leaving for Fontainebleau, the comte d'Artois decided to raze a little house he owns in the Bois de Boulogne, called Bagatelle, and to entirely rebuild, to new plans, a house that would be arranged and furnished in time to give a party for the Queen when the court left Choisy to return to Versailles. At first everyone thought it was absurd to attempt and complete such an undertaking in six or seven weeks. And yet this is just what was done thanks to nine hundred laborers of all kinds, who were hired to work day and night. The most incredible circumstance is that materials were lacking, especially dressed stone, lime, and plaster, and they didn't want to waste time seeking them. So the count ordered his Swiss guards to go about the main highways and halt all the carts they might find loaded with the above-mentioned materials. The cost was paid on the spot, but since the merchandise had already been sold, this method entailed a kind of violence that outraged the public. It is hard to believe that the king tolerates such frivolities, and unfortunately it is supposed that they would not be allowed without the protection afforded by the queen.[39]

It was one of Artois's bold strokes. Ready to risk all, he won the bet, bringing the artists on stage: along with the architect François-Joseph Bélanger, some of the most talented painters, bronzesmiths, and sculptors would create, in a flash, one of the finest masterpieces of French architecture and decorative arts of the late eighteenth century.

PAGE 62
Armand Parfait Prieur, *Bagatelle Viewed from the Garden* (detail), etching, 1778 (Musée Carnavalet – Histoire de Paris, Paris). The comte d'Artois's architect, François-Joseph Bélanger completed construction of the pavilion of Bagatelle in sixty-four days, enabling the count to win his wager with Marie Antoinette.

FACING PAGE
Sphinx on the terrace overlooking the main courtyard. The Egyptian theme, so fashionable during the reign of Louis XVI, recurs often at Bagatelle. Sculpted or painted sphinxes can still be seen today, whereas an obelisk with hieroglyphs and a pharaonic tomb, formerly on the grounds, have vanished.

PAGE 66
"Series of details on the Pavilion of Bagatelle", engraving published in *Recueil d'Architecture Civile* by Jean-Charles Krafft, 1810. The courtyard façade, whose door is flanked by two projecting columns, was enlivened by sculptures in the now-empty niches, whereas the bas-reliefs on the attic story have fortunately survived.

PAGE 67
Claude Fessard Lainé, after Louis-Gabriel Moreau, *The Interior of the Grounds of Bagatelle, Showing the Obelisk and the Waterfall Opposite the Pavilion* (detail), engraving published in the "Isle de France" section of *Vues Pittoresques de la France*, 1818–20, plate 84 (collection of the author).

L
N
M
K
G
H
I
Elévation.
E
Coupe.
F
12 Pieds

Chapter 3

The Château de Bagatelle

A Masterpiece of French Architecture and Interior Decoration

"The whole aspect of the building that I here describe in detail is among the most beautiful of its kind and incontestably one of the finest works of recent French architecture. In both distribution and style, it may serve as an excellent model; one, moreover, that is executed with such neatness and care as to mark the highest degree of perfection in every respect: a testimony to the skill of the artists employed that is rendered yet more admirable by the well-nigh incredible rapidity with which the project was planned and executed."

Friedrich Gilly, "A description of the Villa of Bagatelle, near Paris," *Essays on Architecture 1796–1799*

PARVA SED APTA

The château de Bagatelle built by the comte d'Artois is remarkable both for its highly original architecture and for the beauty and quality of its interior decoration, executed by the finest artists and craftsmen of the day. In 1799 the famous German architect Friedrich Gilly already recognized it as a timeless masterpiece.

In its size, proportions, and landscape setting, Bagatelle is representative of the small country pavilions that sprang up around Paris in the second half of the eighteenth century. Their emergence reflected a growing rejection of Louis-XIV pomp and large, stately salons. Individuals became increasingly concerned with concepts of conviviality, personal happiness, privacy, and a quest for freedom in harmony with nature. A house outside the city fulfilled those aspirations. People dined in small groups in more modest, more practical rooms. Mistresses could be received there in all tranquility. Conversation could flow more freely. "These little houses are a charming idea; mystery devises them, good taste builds them, convenience arranges them, and elegance furnishes their modest rooms. Only the basic necessities are found there, but those necessities are a hundred-fold more delightful than everything superfluous.... Proper behavior is left at the door; privacy serves as a sentinel allowing entry only to pleasure and friendly libertinage."[40]

Perfect illustrations of this phenomenon, in its "royal" version, are the Pavillon Français and the Petit Trianon, both built on the grounds of Versailles. The Pavillon Français was designed by architect Ange Jacques Gabriel for Louis XV and Madame de Pompadour in 1750, intended to serve simultaneously as a refuge for enjoying nature and a place of entertainment. The central space is a circular music room with four large French windows overlooking the garden, an idea copied in the large drawing room at Bagatelle. As architecture historian Jean-Marie Pérouse de Montclos pointed out, this pavilion represented Louis XV's ideal of French style, whose two key features were simplicity and nobility, as Gabriel explained in a letter to Marigny.[41] The king said to the duc de Croÿ, "This is the style in which building should be done."[42]

The Petit Trianon, also by architect Gabriel, is another example of the French classical tradition, its Louis-XVI style in fact being a "Louis-XIV revival style from the Louis-XV era." Built in 1762–64 for Madame de Pompadour once again, the Petit Trianon is a simple pavilion, the elevation on its garden side featuring a row of tall French windows, above which sat a low, upper floor called the attic. This, too, was copied at Bagatelle.

Bagatelle indeed descended from the French "pavilion" tradition. A 1787 tourist guidebook, Luc-Vincent Thiery's *Guide des amateurs et des étrangers voyageurs à Paris*, unwittingly quoted Gabriel when referring to its "simple yet noble architecture."[43] Yet the building's style also reflects a different inspiration: it had a thoroughly British air, as brilliantly interpreted by the architect Bélanger.

François-Joseph Bélanger was born in 1744, one of nineteen children of a luxury-goods dealer. His sister Marie-Anne Adélaïde would marry the draftsman Dugourc, while his brother Louis would become painter to the comte d'Artois and later painter at the court of Sweden.[44] In the early 1760s, Bélanger entered the Académie Royale d'Architecture under the patronage of the comte de Caylus and under the supervision of Julien David Le Roy and Pierre Contant d'Ivry. These three men were the great partisans of "antique" classicism in French decorative arts and architecture in the 1750s and 1760s. The comte de Caylus published an anthology of

PAGES 68–69
Louis Bélanger, *The Bagatelle Pavilion Seen from the Main Entrance*, gouache, 1785 (private collection).

PAGE 71
Courtyard view of the château de Bagatelle. Renovations carried out in the nineteenth century by a rich English collector, the marquess of Hertford, altered Bélanger's original design by raising the roof to make the upper floor more comfortable. By giving the building a façade and proportions typical of the Louis-XVI style of the 1770s, this renovation paradoxically eliminated the touch of Englishness sought by the young comte d'Artois and his architect.

FACING PAGE
The façade seen from the garden. The dome was raised as part of the conversion work done by Lord Hertford.

ABOVE
Claude-Louis Châtelet, *Façade of the Pavilion to be Used for Concerts*, pen and ink, 1786 (Biblioteca Estense Universitaria, Modena). The French Pavilion on the grounds of the château de Versailles, built by Ange Jacques Gabriel for Louis XV and Madame de Pompadour in 1750, was a bucolic retreat as well as a place of entertainment. The idea of a circular living room, with four large French windows giving onto the garden, was the model for the grand salon at Bagatelle.

FACING PAGE
The influence of English architect William Chambers on Bélanger, who designed Bagatelle, seems to have been crucial. These two drawings by Chambers display obvious resemblances to Bagatelle. Top, *Plan for a Casino*, 1765; bottom, *Design for a Hunting Lodge at Roxborough, Co. Tyrone*, 1768 (Victoria and Albert Museum, London).

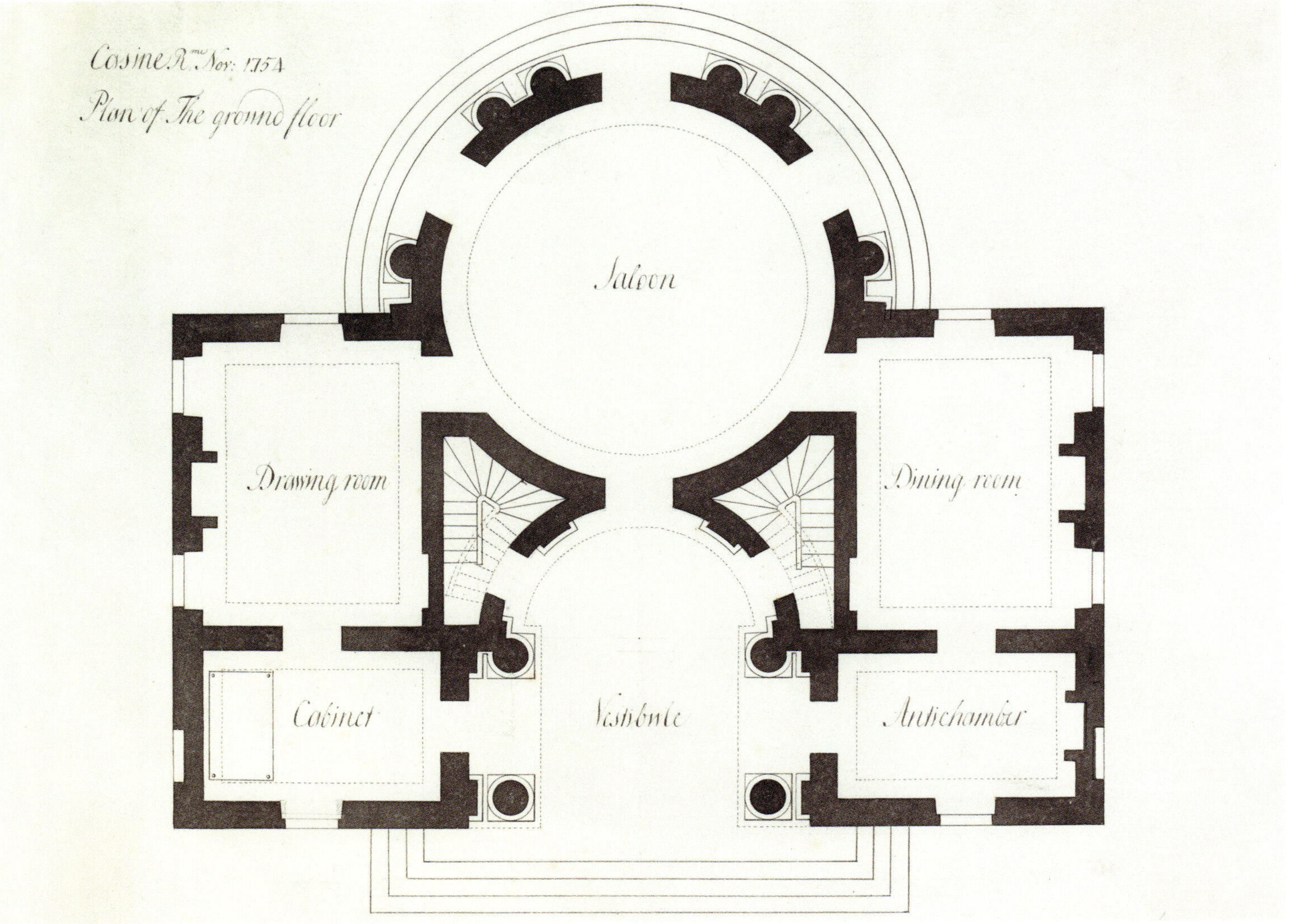

Cosine R.me Nov: 1754
Plan of The ground floor

Saloon

Drawing room

Dining room

Cabinet

Vestibule

Antichamber

5 10 15 20 25 ft

Egyptian, Etruscan, Greek, and Roman antiquities from 1752 to 1765, while Le Roy published a second edition of his book on the ruins of the finest buildings in Greece in 1770. These two monumental publications constituted a watershed in the exploration and dissemination of the aesthetics of antiquity and the neoclassical revival in France. Above all, in the late 1760s Le Roy served as an adviser to Marc René de Voyer de Paulmy d'Argenson, marquis de Voyer, on the building of the Orléans chancellery and the hôtel de Voyer, two construction projects being supervised by Charles de Wailly. Voyer and Le Roy were both friendly with, and correspondents of, the architect William Chambers, who began his career in Paris in 1749 before becoming the leading architect for King George III of Great Britain.

After finishing at the Académie Royale, from 1766 Bélanger traveled several times to England, and the very special inflection we sense at Bagatelle was probably due to those voyages and to the Palladian revival that was highly fashionable on the other side of the Channel at the time. We know that Chambers received Bélanger at least once in 1767, and the following year Bélanger dedicated to him a drawing of the façade of the hôtel de Brancas for the comte de Lauraguais: "Dedicated to Monsieur William Chambers by his most humble servant, Bélanger."[45] Their encounter seems to have had a decisive impact on the design of Bagatelle.

As Giles Worsley wrote, "Chambers was not immune to the influence of other first and second-generation neo-Palladians. In his unexecuted *Design for a Hunting Lodge at Roxborough, Co. Tyrone* (1768), Chambers designed a pyramidal cube in the manner of Roger Morris, perhaps inspired by his own house at Whitton which Morris had designed."[46] Chambers's drawing for the Roxborough hunting lodge, as well as a 1765 "Casino in the Style of Peruzzi," bears striking similarities with Bagatelle, notably in the elevation of the main façade and the triangular shape of the roof of the hunting lodge. The plan for another casino in the Chambers archives is very similar to the one that Bélanger adopted for Bagatelle, with a large round drawing room with three large French windows (although lacking the antechambers flanking it at Bagatelle), a dining room and a drawing room on either side, and a rectangular entrance hall with a single, central staircase.[47] The ensemble was then capped by a domed cupola. A dome can also be found at Chiswick House, an early example of the English Palladian revival. Designed by the earl of Burlington in 1729, it combines a cupola with triangular roof, as seen in the comte d'Artois's pleasure pavilion.

Bagatelle thus represents a successful marriage of French tradition with English-Palladianism as perfectly orchestrated by Bélanger: a French pavilion set on a terrace, a simple façade with three windows, ground-level entrance, small upper floor, triangular—rather than flat—roof underscoring the "bare," compact nature of the building, very limited use of columns, and a large, Burlington-style dome.

It is now time to enter the pavilion. Here we find a Louis-XVI interior in which French tradition is combined with the "Greek style" that is then all the rage, but with the marked presence of decorative grotesques that lighten, moderate, and "feminize" what might have been otherwise too strict an aspect of this setting. What is there to admire in the Louis-XVI style? The correct proportions, the beautiful design, the quality of materials, and the refined finish—an overall impression of harmony and elegance. What do the grotesques contribute? Forms that evoke nature and femininity, gracefulness, the mysteries of ancient mythology, spring-like colors,

FACING PAGE
Elevation of the Courtyard Façade of Bagatelle, ink and wash, late eighteenth century, drawing by Bélanger's studio, approved by the comte d'Artois (Bibliothèque Nationale de France).

PAGES 78–79
Perspective View of Bagatelle, pen and ink and color wash, late eighteenth century, cartouche from the *Carte des chasses de Monseigneur le comte d'Artois* (Bibliothèque Historique de la Ville de Paris).

bon

VUE PERSPECTIVE

DE BAGATELLE.

Bon

Façade du Pavillon de Bagatelle côté du jardin

Six Toises

whimsical animals, and unknown worlds that beckon—a call to the imagination, a touch of lightness and folly.

Both this elegance and this lightness are found at Bagatelle thanks to the architect's many talents. Bélanger's ability to compose interiors that are particularly harmonious was combined with his great experience as a designer of decorative arts. He developed the former talent while working, from 1767 onward, for the Revels, the office in the royal household responsible for festivities and ceremonies at court. As a "designer of models," Bélanger created the famous jewelry chest for Marie Antoinette when she was still the dauphine,[48] and he designed many gilt-bronze objects executed by goldsmith Pierre Gouthière for the duc d'Aumont and the duchesse de Mazarin. Thanks to the benevolent patronage of actress Sophie Arnould, whom he met at the celebrations for the marriage of Louis XVI and Marie Antoinette, Bélanger was then named, in 1770, designer to the comte de Provence. Then, in 1777, he paid 36,000 livres to acquire the office of first architect to the comte d'Artois.

Thanks to Bélanger, Bagatelle was endowed with the finest French decorative arts of the 1770s and 1780s: paintings on walls and ceilings, teeming grotesques of Roman inspiration, magnificent gilt-bronze items (clocks, candelabra, andirons, lanterns), elegant, perfectly proportioned furniture (either in mahogany or gilded and painted wood), the finest fabrics and tapestries, and finally, sculptures and paintings by the best artists of the day, such as Hubert Robert.

The layout of the château is simple. On the ground floor, one enters from the courtyard via a vestibule that leads to the dining room on the left and the billiard room on the right, while straight ahead is a staircase leading to the upper floor. On the garden side, a round music room occupies the central space, with its grand domed ceiling and magnificent decorative panels. To the left of the music room is the so-called Hubert Robert bathroom, to the right, the Callet boudoir. In addition to doors leading to those two rooms, the large music room has five other openings: two doors leading to the dining room (on the left) and the billiard room (on the right), and three large French windows overlooking the garden, imbuing it with the light and colors of nature, as per the tradition of French pavilions.

Upstairs, on the courtyard side, was the bedroom of the comte d'Artois as well as his study and an antechamber, and finally, the boudoir of the private upstairs apartment opposite. On the right was the lodging of the captain of the guards, including a bedroom overlooking the courtyard and two antechambers toward the garden. In the middle was lodging for attendants, overlooking the courtyard.

Without necessarily describing every feature of the décor, it is important to imagine the overall impression made on visitors. The floors were of marble or oak, depending on the room's purpose. The doors and wall panels were painted in veined wood or colored marble (white, pink, and yellow) or grotesques, sometimes with gilded frames. The fireplaces were of marble and gilt bronze, and the dining room was also adorned with a large, imitation-porphyry basin—a kind of fountain that the comte d'Artois perhaps used to cool his champagne. It made a big impression on visitors and was described in a contemporary guidebook as "a large basin placed in front of a mirror, with water spouting from two dolphins. The mirror doubling the features of this fountain seem to make it whole, standing alone in the middle of a room extended by reflection, which produces a delightful surprise."[49]

FACING PAGE
Garden Façade of Bagatelle, ink and wash, late eighteenth century, drawing by Bélanger's studio, approved by the comte d'Artois (Bibliothèque Nationale de France). A blend of French tradition and English-style Palladian revival, the Bagatelle pavilion featured a simple, spare façade on the courtyard side but a large, Burlington-type dome on the garden side.

PAGES 82–83
François-Joseph Bélanger, *Bagatelle: Plan of the Ground Floor*, ink and wash (Bibliothèque Nationale de France). In his account in a *Voyage à Paris en 1782*, a gentlemen from Brittany wrote that, "The pavilion is everything that sensual pleasure can most lavishly devise: the apartments are oval, composed of five ground-floor rooms and five above, all glassed and richly decorated with paintings."

Jardin.

Terrasse.

Bains.

Sal

Parterre

au Couchant.

Salle à manger.

Dégr

Vestib

Chemin de St Cloud à St Denis.

Terrasse.

Cour

Terrasse basse.

Jardin.

Terrasse.

Boudoir.

Salle

de Billard.

Couloir.

Parterre

au Levant.

Bois de Boulogne.

Terrasse.

Six Toises.

Terrasse basse.

ABOVE
The spiral staircase leading to the boudoirs upstairs is lit from above. Taking up little space, it is suited to the modest dimensions of the pavilion. "The mahogany staircase is highly singular, and of a boldness that will startle connoisseurs," noted the Bachaumont memoirs.

FACING PAGE
Adorned with Ionic columns of stucco designed to imitate pink granite, the entrance hall is decorated in a spare, neoclassical style. The only surviving furniture is a round, garland-draped stove on which stood a figured candelabra (now replaced by a bust of Richard Wallace).

The dining-room ceiling was entirely painted in colored compartments with a central, imitation-cameo depiction of the wedding of Psyche, while the walls, punctuated with pilasters, were of ancient yellow marble. The billiard-room ceiling was similar, but in an almost Pompeiian mode. A large central panel featuring a cameo-like head of Mercury was flanked by two large panels with grotesques, scrollwork, and cameos of the comte d'Artois's monogram, as well as four corner panels with cameos of chariot races—the whole in color. The effect was certainly spectacular, as witnessed by a preparatory drawing for the dining-room ceiling now in the Metropolitan Museum of Art in New York[50] (see pp. 114–15).

The interior decoration at Bagatelle is characterized by the successful marriage of the grand classical style with the refinement and lightness of painted decoration.[51] The better to appreciate this harmony, we should remember that such a combination did not go without saying—quite the contrary. Classicism often meant a rejection of swirls, whimsical animals, and other imaginary décors, a rejection already at work in ancient Rome. Thus Vitruvius, writing in the first century BCE, criticized their fantasy and lack of realism in what almost sounds like a description of the interior of Bagatelle:

> We now have fresco paintings of monstrosities, rather than truthful representations of definite things. For instance, [we see] ... candelabra supporting representations of shrines, and on top of their pediments numerous tender stalks and volutes growing up from the roots and having human figures senselessly seated upon them; sometimes stalks having only half-length figures, some with human heads, others with the heads of animals. Such things do not exist and cannot exist and never have existed.[52]

Ever since the rediscovery of the Domus Aurea in Rome in the Renaissance, grotesques were recognized as a key feature of interior decoration in antiquity, and that was further confirmed by the excavations at Herculaneum in 1730–40. Yet it is only with the pioneering designers of the 1760s that they made their triumphal return. Back in 1515, Raphael had already reconciled grotesques with the "strict" taste of antiquity in his Loggias at the Vatican, imposing an order and organization on them that proved more compatible with the style of the 1760s and 1770s. As Claude Henri Watelet wrote in the eighteenth-century *Encylopédie*, "the wild inventiveness of grotesques is, as it were, neutralized by the symmetry, elegant forms, pleasant choice of subjects, and unexaggerated lightness of arrangement." Watelet viewed Raphael's paintings in the Loggias as the model for a "modern school of grotesques for the new generation of architects and decorators."[53]

Bélanger never had an opportunity to go to Rome and he never personally saw the ruins of the Domus Aurea or Raphael's Loggias. Grotesques nevertheless played a central role in his aesthetic realm. They had already appeared in many Paris residences in the late 1760s, including the mansion of the marquis de Voyer, as well as in Bélanger's first major project, the hôtel de Brancas, in 1768. Publishers of engravings in France began issuing new reproductions of the Loggias, and the first plates of the complete edition sponsored by Pope Clement XIII, *Le Loggie de Rafaele nel Vaticano*, were also available in Paris. Furthermore, Bélanger benefited from the Roman experiences of colleagues—Jean-Démosthène Dugourc, his brother-in-law, had lived in Rome in the 1760s, while Nicolas Lhuillier, the sculptor at Bagatelle, had numerous anthologies

FACING PAGE
Located to the left of the music room, the so-called Hubert Robert bathroom was adorned with a set of paintings by Robert, whose originals are now in the Metropolitan Museum, New York. The painting on the door panel dates from the nineteenth century.

PAGES 88–91
The six paintings by Robert that once decorated the count's bathroom were still in Bagatelle in 1797, but were sold at auction in 1808. They were acquired by J.P. Morgan, who bequeathed them to the Metropolitan Museum of Art in New York in 1917. On the other side of the music room, Antoine-François Callet delivered six mythological paintings for the adjacent boudoir. While the Callet paintings have a clear erotic message, Hubert Robert's works appeal more subtly to the visitors' voyeurism. Page 88: *The Bathing Pool*. Page 89: *Traveling Musicians*.

ABOVE, LEFT
The Fountain.

ABOVE, RIGHT
The Dance.

ABOVE, LEFT
The Swing.

ABOVE
The Entrance of a Cave, oil on canvas
(All Metropolitan Museum of Art, New York).

of grotesques in his library. The largely intact decoration in the music room is still a wonderful, Loggia-inspired feast for the eyes. A contemporary account described it as "Italian in style; it is a rotunda, very fine in elevation, decorated with mirrors and bas-reliefs showing grotesques and various allegorical figures. These bas-reliefs are of exquisite taste, standing out against the ground in soft colors, whose harmonious tones produce, along with the other paintings and color in the room, a simultaneously noble, elegant, and pleasant overall effect."[54]

The contractor's detailed invoice for Lhuillier's work provides a perfect description that is still valid today:

> [Lhuillier] executed two designs of different composition, one with a figure of Harmony holding a lyre, seated on a three-legged chair composed of dolphins adorned with boughs of laurel; on the figure's head is a vase.... [T]he other design is also composed of a seated figure, here on a globe set on a pedestal with intertwining snakes and laurel boughs; the figure blows on a sea trumpet, while on her head is a basket of fruit and flowers from which emerge garlands to which horns are attached.[55]

The doors of the two ground-level boudoirs, as well as the decoration of the boudoir in the private apartment upstairs, extend the charm of these light, feminine grotesques. Most exceptionally, the château still retains part of this original décor, including paintings by Jean-Marie Dusseaux, *Venus as a Pilgrim* and *Cupid on the Hunt*.

In addition to the wall decoration, gilt bronze-work and furnishings echoed these grotesque motifs all the while adding a more classical, achitectural, and even military touch, notably by alluding to the count's rank of colonel-general of the Swiss Guards.

Gilt bronze-work was a key aspect of craft excellence in eighteenth-century France, and all three of the leading bronze gilders under Louis XVI—Pierre Gouthière, François Rémond, and Philippe Thomire—worked at Bagatelle for the comte d'Artois.[56] Many clocks designed by Bélanger for the pavilion became highly popular and were often copied. Such was the sphinx clock made for the music room, which reflected the patterns on one of Lhuillier's panels, and whose historic description stresses the outstanding quality of its execution:

> This clock is richly decorated with symbols, boughs of lilac and other flowers and fruit, of superior execution. Two winged sphinxes, richly draped and supported by the base, hold the clock that is set on a pillow adorned and supported by the tails of the sphinxes and other embroidery; the plinth is architectural, decorated at its round ends by rich garlands of fruit and flowers; the front of this plinth is adorned with a superb recessed frieze of signs of the zodiac, whose beautiful finish entailed prodigious cost; the whole stands on eight elongated, fluted, chased balls. Never has bronze been finished with so much care as the ornaments of this case, which are extremely detailed and of considerable size; they were gilded with equal care, requiring prodigious expenditure unmatched by any other work of this size.[57]

Another remarkable clock was based on "a truncated fluted column of white marble, adorned with garlands, on which is set a richly decorated bronze globe engraved with the various parts of the world; this globe is accompanied by clouds and two draped children bearing stars which

PAGES 92–93
Jean-Démosthène Dugoure, *The Garden Façade of Bagatelle*, pen and black ink, watercolor, over traces of black chalk, 1779 (Metropolitan Museum of Art, New York).

FACING PAGE
View of the painted dome of the music room. Despite nineteenth- and twentieth-century modifications, the neoclassical spirit of the original decoration remains intact.

PAGE 96
Bagatelle's main room—the music room—is a rotunda with three large French windows leading to the garden. Drenched in light, it has retained its Louis-XVI decoration, in which panels of grotesques impart life to strict neoclassical lines. It is connected to a dining room on the left, and to a billiard room on the right.

"Italian in style; it is a rotunda, very fine in elevation, decorated with mirrors and bas-reliefs showing grotesques and various allegorical figures. These bas-reliefs are of exquisite taste, standing out against the ground in soft colors, whose harmonious tones produce, along with the other paintings and color in the room, a simultaneously noble, elegant and pleasant overall effect."

Vues pittoresques: Plans et descriptions des principaux jardins anglais qui sont en France, c. 1780–85

FACING PAGE
Detail of the cornices above the French windows in the music room, draped with richly trimmed fabric placed there in the late twentieth century.

ABOVE
The wall panels in the music room have retained their stucco decoration sculpted by Lhuillier to designs by Bélanger inspired by the Loggias of Raphael in the Vatican. Two designs alternate. Here, Harmony is seated on a tripod and plays the lyre; the other design shows an allegorical figure seated on a globe of the earth and blowing a sea-themed trumpet (see page 181).

ABOVE
Chairs that once furnished the bedroom of the comte d'Artois at Bagatelle. Made by cabinetmaker Georges Jacob and carved by Jean-Baptiste Rode and Daniel Aubert, this furniture—bearing Bagatelle's branded mark—resurfaced on the art market in the years 1990–2000. Today they are part of a private collection, along with a chest belonging to the same set.

FACING PAGE
The carved decoration, incorporating fasces, laurel leaves, clubs, and arrows, is described in Rode's invoice for the work. The war-like theme of the count's bedroom reflected his rank of colonel-general of the Swiss Guards.

FACING PAGE
Armchair stamped Georges Jacob with Bagatelle's branded mark. Originally designed for one of the ground-floor boudoirs, this armchair was bought by the Fondation Mansart in 2021 thanks to the patronage of the Foundation La Marck.

ABOVE
The rich carving testifies to the outstanding quality of the furniture supplied to the comte d'Artois and the lavish expense it required. The chair still bears the traces of royal fleur-de-lis, effaced during the Revolution. It was originally upholstered in an "English-green *gros de tours* [silk taffeta]."

can be detached. They represent dawn, tearing away the veil of night. This clock was very difficult to make. It shows the hours and minutes, for all parts of the world, and on the globe are circles representing the equator."[58] The original clock of white marble has been lost, but other versions exist, such as one of gray marble, auctioned in 2020.

Some of the andirons would also become classic, like one "composed of two turtle doves set on clouds in which are bows, quivers, and torches,"[59] as well as the sphinx andirons in the music salon that imitated a Dusseaux motif on the door of the boudoir in the private apartment above, and of which a version exists in the château de Versailles.

Finally, among the nine fireplaces attributed to Gouthière and listed in the catalogue raisonné of his work,[60] three were delivered to Madame du Barry at Fontainebleau, two were ordered by Marie Antoinette and Louis XVI, one was delivered to the duchesse de Mazarin, and three went to Bagatelle for the comte d'Artois. These last three fireplaces, unfortunately stolen in the 1980s, are a lost testament to of the outstanding quality of the Bagatelle's interior decoration.

Furniture had been another realm of excellence in French decorative arts since the late seventeenth century. The most magnificent commissions and most beautiful pieces were to be found at the French court, which attracted many talented artisans from Germany and the Netherlands. There were cabinetmakers, who specialized in wood veneering and who made tables, chests of drawers, elaborate desks, and writing cabinets, while joiners worked the solid wood and made chairs, armchairs, stools, and beds, as well as pier tables. The solid wood on these articles of joinery would be carved and then painted or gilded, depending on use and period.

Given the size of Bagatelle, there were few large pieces of cabinetwork—no mention is made of a single large desk. Only two large chests of drawers made by Stockel were supplied for the bedrooms[61] and a few small tables and other items of cabinetmaking were delivered by Denizot.

Joinery is another story. For the château alone, Georges Jacob supplied eighteen stools, eighty-five chairs, twenty-five armchairs, nine sofas, ottomans and upholstered benches, eight screens, and five beds. The masterpieces produced for Bagatelle included the chairs and armchairs for the music room, the furniture for the comte d'Artois's bedroom, and the "king's armchair" made specially for a visit by Louis XVI in 1784. Also outstanding were the large *bergère* chairs and the fire screen for the music room, delivered by Jean-Baptiste Boulard. Three types of artisan participated in the making of these masterworks: the joiner, the carver, and the gilder. The carving is particularly complex and refined—the carver Jean-Baptiste Rode, who worked for Bagatelle, was the highest paid craftsman.

Several pieces of the original furniture survive: one of the large *bergères* delivered by Boulard (now in the Mobilier National in Paris), an armchair and a folding screen (now in Waddesdon Manor),[62] and a set of six chairs that once belonged to the comtesse Greffulhe (now in a private collection).[63] A pair of armchairs executed in a very similar spirit by the same team—Jacob, Rode, and the same gilder, Ramier—for the comte d'Artois's Turkish boudoir in the Temple is now in the Louvre's collection.[64] The famous royal armchair at Bagatelle, plus two chairs from the comte d'Artois's bedroom, also survive and are in private hands.[65]

The bedroom merits special attention: fabrics reigned supreme and the furniture was particularly original and arresting. The designs for it, now in the Bibliothèque Nationale,

FACING PAGE
The comte d'Artois's private apartment upstairs—five bedrooms, three antechambers, and two private rooms—have survived, but these small rooms were profoundly altered when their ceilings were raised in 1860. While awaiting imminent restoration, two delicate paintings by Jean-Marie Dusseaux—*Cupid on the Hunt* (shown here) and *Venus as a Pilgrim*—still adorn the door panels.

constitute some of the best-known examples of the day, although the artisans' work does not exactly match them. The famous Bachaumont memoirs patiently take the visitor on a tour:

> The mahogany staircase is highly singular, and of a boldness that will startle connoisseurs, being so narrow that one cannot give one's hand to a Lady. This staircase climbs to the few bedrooms above. The one for the prince, in which he never lived, is truly remarkable, for everything suggests military quarters: the pilasters are decorated with clusters of arms crowned by a helmet; the sideposts of the mantelpiece are two cannon barrels set on their breeches; the andirons take the form of cannon balls, bombs, grenades; the wall lights are hunting horns.[66]

The result was highly original, and probably more decorative than functional. This stately bedroom was not where trysts took place. Instead, there was a famous "secret" boudoir located between the count's bathroom and his first antechamber.[67] From the outside, the château's two rows of windows give no hint of the existence of this mezzanine level, designed for discretion. A drawing attributed to Bélanger, purchased by the Amis du Château de Bagatelle in the 1980s, appears to be a sketch of it. In his memoirs, Général Thiébault referred to his many visits to Bagatelle and recounted his experience of the premises. "I had received an invitation from the prince d'Hénin to go there whenever I wished. I often took ladies and was sometimes amused by the awkwardness caused by a boudoir which—in addition to some highly unorthodox paintings—had a floor, walls, and ceiling all of mirror, and where the ladies had no other option but to hastily turn their dress into a kind of pantaloon." Thiébault concluded, leaving aside any ambiguity: "There would be no end to detailed description of this voluptuous setting, in truth quite small yet sufficient to worship of the god to whom it was dedicated, and which would be, forever, so aptly designed by the motto *Parva sed apta* ["Small but suitable"], placed over the entrance to the ultimate bastion."[68]

Bachaumont's memoirs confirm the existence of this "place of worship": "The boudoir displayed all kinds of voluptuous paintings by our modern masters—Greuze, Fragonard, Lagrenée, etc. A bed of roses and mirrors that repeated the positions of the lovers on all sides, however, simply constituted what can be seen in other châteaux, for example in the king's pavilion."[69]

This gave rise to a veritable legend. The vicomte de Reiset, whose ancestors were likely witnesses, reported as much in his 1906 biography of the duchesse de Berry:

> For a long time the public spoke only of the flirtatious parties given by the comte d'Artois at Bagatelle, and the rumors concerned above all a notorious boudoir whose ceiling, walls, and even floor were entirely covered in mirrors. If the legend is to be believed, they were arranged so ingeniously that the imprudent ladies who ventured there soon repented of their curiosity, and their consternation became extreme once they realized how indiscreet were all these mirrors, revealing even their most private charms.[70]

This installation of mirrors was not unique. In the 1760s the architect Étienne Louis Boullée designed a Turkish boudoir for François Racine de Monville's lavish Paris residence on rue d'Anjou-Saint-Honoré.[71] As described by Dufort de Cheverny in his memoirs, "Everything was

FACING PAGE, TOP
Georges-Louis Le Rouge, after François-Joseph Bélanger, *The Comte d'Artois's Bedroom at Bagatelle, Fireplace End*, colored print (Bibliothèque Nationale de France). Although the bedroom created for the comte d'Artois somewhat differed from Bélanger's original design, its interior decoration became a landmark of the Louis-XVI style, and was notably copied at the Lambert mansion.

FACING PAGE, BOTTOM
The fireplace in the comte d'Artois's bedroom at Bagatelle, photographed by Jean Barry in 1902 (Musée Carnavalet – Histoire de Paris, Paris). To match the army-tent-themed interior, the fireplace was flanked by two cannon barrels of blue Turquin marble adorned with bronzes by Pierre Gouthière, stolen in the 1980s.

Septembre 1902

Bagatelle. Cheminée de l'ancienne chambre du Comte d'Artois.

"For a long time the public spoke only of the flirtatious parties given by the comte d'Artois at Bagatelle, and the rumors concerned above all a notorious boudoir whose ceiling, walls, and even floor were entirely covered in mirrors."

Vicomte de Reiset

made of mirror, with no windows; light came from glass overhead; a projecting balustrade in the finest taste, behind which hid a tiny orchestra, curved above this salon, which was fitted with a very thick Turkish carpet; there reigned a divan of crimson velvet with gold fringe…; the doors to this delightful lair closed easily on sliders that followed the shape of the salon; a hidden button on the wall opened them with marvelous promptness."[72] From October 1776 to March 1777 Boullée installed another Turkish boudoir, this time for the comte d'Artois's residence at the Temple, but resigned the job a few months later in favor of Bélanger,[73] who therefore copied the idea of a mirrored boudoir at Bagatelle.

Another, no less significant, example was cited in Antoine Caillot's memoirs, this time making its purpose even more explicit:

> In 1788, it was with the liveliest admiration that we visited Mademoiselle Dervieux's little house on rue Chantereine. The furniture in the bedroom had cost over 36,000 francs, one-third of that sum for the bed alone. The sides, ceiling, and floor of the boudoir were adorned with mirrors between which no gap existed. The floor mirrors of this little temple of Venus were strewn with pillows used for amorous combat. Thus two lovers, in their voluptuous embraces, could gaze upon themselves in every position. The concierge who guided us said that one lord, of the highest rank, often came to this sanctuary to frolic with the actress.[74]

Mademoiselle Dervieux's famous house, built by Alexandre Théodore Brongniart in 1777,[75] was largely revamped by Bélanger when he became the owner's lover. In 1788, the ballerina and courtesan was at the height of her glory and the comte d'Artois, like many others, was one of her lovers at the time.[76] Perhaps he was the lord mentioned in Caillot's memoirs. From the Turkish boudoir at the Temple to Chantereine, via Bagatelle, the same comforts and familiar surroundings are found thanks to the good offices of Boullée and Bélanger.

PAGE 108
Detail of fabric trimming in the bedroom alcove.

PAGE 109
Jean-Démosthène Dugourc, *The Lovers Espied*, pen and India ink, watercolor on paper (private collection). Dugourc was Bélanger's brother-in-law and worked with the latter decorating the duchesse de Mazarin's residence as well as Artois's pavilion. Two baldly erotic drawings by Dugourc (here and page 113) show libertine activities in lavish settings that, while not categorically identifiable, recall the interiors at Bagatelle.

FACING PAGE
Jean-Michel Moreau, *Le Souper Fin* (A Dainty Supper), black ink, brown wash, and graphite on paper, 1777 (Waddesdon Manor, Buckinghamshire). This drawing evokes the dinners held by the comte d'Artois at Bagatelle, which, "without being absolutely indecent, are nevertheless much too gay," according to the Austrian ambassador's warning to Empress Maria Theresa.

ABOVE
Jean-Baptiste and Henry Lepaute, clockmakers; Pierre Gouthière, bronzesmith; Louis-Simon Boizot, sculptor; François-Joseph Bélanger, designer, *Sphinx Mantel Clock*, c. 1783, gilt bronze, marble (Wallace Collection, London). This is the same model delivered to Bagatelle in 1781, of which several versions survive, including one now at the Trianon in Versailles (Mobilier National, Paris).

FACING PAGE
Jean-Démosthène Dugourc, *The Obliging Lady Friend*, pen and India ink, watercolor on paper (private collection). The sphinx mantel clock on the fireplace is similar to the one in Bagatelle's music room at the time.

PAGES 114–15
François-Joseph Bélanger, *Ceiling of the Dining-Room of the Bagatelle Pavilion*, pencil, pen and ink, wash (Metropolitan Museum of Art, New York). The compartmentalized ceiling decoration is arrayed around a central cameo showing the wedding of Psyche.

Plafond De la Salle d

Manger, De Bagatelle. Belanger

Chapter 4

French Fêtes in an English-Style Garden

Recollections of a Scotsman

"A garden in the English taste
is artfully exceeded in this place.
Its laws, by Bélanger laid down
the better nature to adorn,
ensure that all sides interlace
woods and lawns, with flowers graced.
Apollo here finds new renown,
resembling quite Artois of face.
Choice pleasures does the god bring 'round,
and hence this garden, by his immortal voice
called Bagatelle, in modest jest
surpasses kingly gardens best."

Antoine-Marin Lemierre

In 1982, the well-known English historian of architecture and gardens, David Watkins, published *The English Vision: The Picturesque in Architecture, Landscape and Garden Design*. In explaining the thoroughly British concept of "the picturesque," he unexpectedly took the landscaped grounds of Bagatelle as an example. "The picturesque thus represents the triumph of illusion in which architecture resembles scenery, gardens resemble paintings, and the natural landscape is assessed and criticized ... as though it had been devised by a painter."[77] Watkins went on to quote the Scottish botanist and landscape gardener Thomas Blaikie, who designed the grounds at Bagatelle in conjunction with Bélanger, and who recounted the following anecdote, in which a wall appeared to fall flat at the wave of a magic wand:

> [T]he 20th May [1780] the count gave a great fete at Bagatelle to the King and Queen and the court which was at this time at La Muette; here was the Superbe Band of Musick [*sic, passim*] placed upon a scaffold on a thicket of trees which as the company walked round to see the Gardins played; ... on the further side toward Longchamp there was erected a Pyramide by which was a Marble tomb; this part of the wood being neuly taken in to the grounds there remained the wall of the bois de Boulogne and to rendre this scene More agreable Mr. Bélanger had an invention which made a Singulare effect by undermining the wall on the outside and placing people with ropes to pull the wall down at a word; at this pyramide there was an acteur who acted the part of a Majician who asked there Majestys how they liked the Gardins and what a beautfull vue there was towards the plaine if that wall did not obstruct it, but that there Majestys need only give the word that he with his inchanting wand would make that wall dissapear; the queen not knowing told him with a Laugh "Very well I should wish to see it dissapear" and in the instant the signal was given and above 200 yards oposite where the company stood fell flat to the ground which surprised them all.[78]

Watkins added that, "Make-believe and surprise also played a vital role in the Picturesque."[79] Surprise was that "ah ha!"[80]—or "ha-ha!"—moment, when the curtains were drawn; or when, thanks to Bélanger's stratagem, the wall tumbled to reveal the view beyond.

Although the effect created by Bélanger was indeed "picturesque," the grounds of Bagatelle were not the latest British fashion. Rather, they were a "French-style" English garden. An explanation of that distinction requires a brief review of English landscape gardening in the eighteenth century, as encapsulated by three key phases: the "William Temple" moment of a return to nature, the "William Chambers" moment of "Anglo-Chinois" gardens, and the "Capability Brown" moment of vast green lawns.[81]

In 1692, William Temple published *Upon the Gardens of Epicurus*, which was translated into the French the following year.

> Among us, the beauty of building and planting is placed chiefly in some certain proportions, symmetries, or uniformities; our walks and our trees ranged so as to answer one another, and at exact distances. The Chinese scorn this way of planting, and say a boy that can tell a hundred may plant walks of trees in straight lines, and over against one another, and to what length and extent he pleases. But their greatest reach of imagination is employed in contriving figures where the beauty shall be great, and strike the eye, but without any order or disposition of parts that shall be commonly or easily observed. And though we have hardly any notion of this sort of beauty, yet they have a particular word to express it; and where they find it hit their eye at first sight, they say the *Sharawadgi* is fine or is admirable.[82]

PAGE 117
Modern view of the "Anglo-Chinois" grounds at Bagatelle, designed by Scottish landscape gardener Thomas Blaikie in conjunction with Bélanger. Enlargement and modifications during the Second Empire managed to retain the spirit of the place.

FACING PAGE
Bernd H. Dams and Andrew Zega, after Jean-Charles Krafft, *The Philosopher's Pavilion at Bagatelle*, watercolor, 1994 (private collection). Like most of the follies on the grounds of Bagatelle, the "philosopher's pavilion" is no longer extant; the little Gothic structure was reached by a staircase protected by a parasol.

Seen from the perspective of China and India, order and symmetry were disparaged as "artificial" and rejected in favor of a return to nature. One no longer sought to dominate nature, but to imitate it. The question was not so much to shape a landscape according to a predefined vision external to it, but instead to reveal the "spirit of the place." Contemplation, grace, and serenity were the anticipated products of this return to "primal" nature, as loftily expressed in 1709 by Anthony Ashley Cooper, Earl of Shaftsbury, in *The Moralist*: "Ye Fields and Wood, my Refuge from the toilsome World of Business, receive me in your quiet Sanctuarys, and favour my Retreat and thoughtful Solitude.... O Glorious Nature! Supremely fair and sovereignly Good! All-loving and All-lovely, All-Divine! Whose Looks are so becoming, and of such Infinite Grace; whose Study brings such Wisdom and whose Contemplation such Delight!"[83]

As charming as this idyllic vision may be, it nevertheless requires the work of a gardener, who cannot abandon nature to its own devices. Therefore human intervention, and even the use of artifice, steadily returned. Nature could not remain naked, but needed to be attired. The picturesque required staging.

That vision was defended by William Chambers in three famous publications: *Designs of Chinese Buildings ... To which is Annexed a Description of Their Temples, House, Gardens etc.*, in 1757; *Plans, Elevations, Sections and Perspective Views of the Gardens and Building at Kew in Surrey*, which he produced for the Princess of Wales in 1767; and finally, *Dissertation on Oriental Gardening*, published in 1772. Rapidly translated and distributed in France, his books had a considerable impact. During this Chambers moment, "a gardener had to differ from ordinary nature the way a heroic poem differs from a prose account. Gardeners had to give free rein to their imagination, like poets, and even soar beyond the limits of reality."[84]

Transfiguration was the byword of what the French call "Anglo-Chinois" gardens, which evolved into a series of "scenes" combining plants, rocks, water features, bridges, and sometimes "follies." Follies were "artificial" buildings, often small, designed to evoke a season, an exotic location (such as a Chinese pagoda), an idea (temple of love or truth, etc.), or even, more simply, antiquity (the craze for fake ruins). A "picturesque" landscape became a collection of pictures, each one telling a story. When strolling through the grounds, one travels from one world to another, from one poetic realm to another, from one feeling to another. Nature as "transfigured" by Chambers speaks to us of love, of beauty, of nostalgia for a bygone era.

The history of English-style landscape gardening did not end there, however. The use of artifice, the proliferation of grottoes and follies of all kinds, the overly striking contrasts between scenes, and overloaded senses and meanings, all went out of fashion. A simplification and re-naturalization of landscape occurred in a return to Temple's original ideas. This was the great moment of glory for Capability Brown. Specializing in vast spaces, he became the most sought-after gardener of the landed gentry in George III's kingdom. An uninterrupted view, vast sloping lawn, indispensable water feature, and long, winding path up to the stately home became mandatory. The appeal of regular features and gentle nature returned. A soft smoothness had already been lauded by Edmund Burke in his famous *Philosophical Inquiry into the Origin of our Ideas of the Sublime and the Beautiful* in 1757: "A quality so essential to beauty that I do not recollect anything so beautiful that is not smooth. In trees and flowers, smooth leaves are beautiful; smooth slopes of earth in gardens; smooth streams in the landscape."[85]

FACING PAGE
Louis-Gabriel Moreau, *The Waterfall Bridge and Hermitage on the Grounds of Bagatelle*, gouache, 1785 (private collection). Four gouaches painted in 1785 by Louis Bélanger (the architect's brother) and Louis-Gabriel Moreau reveal the beauty of the grounds at Bagatelle, which in the late eighteenth century became a favorite spot for an outing among Parisians.

PAGE 122
Georges-Louis Le Rouge, *The Grounds of Bagatelle, Dedicated to the Comte d'Artois, Brother of the King*, etching, 1784 (Bibliothèque Nationale de France). People marveled at the complex design of the grounds of Bagatelle, where flowerbeds, groves, and sloping lawns were crisscrossed by winding paths and snaking streams, and punctuated by ponds and waterfalls, rocks and grottoes. Dotted with bridges, exotic pavilions, and follies, they were certain to enchant a stroller.

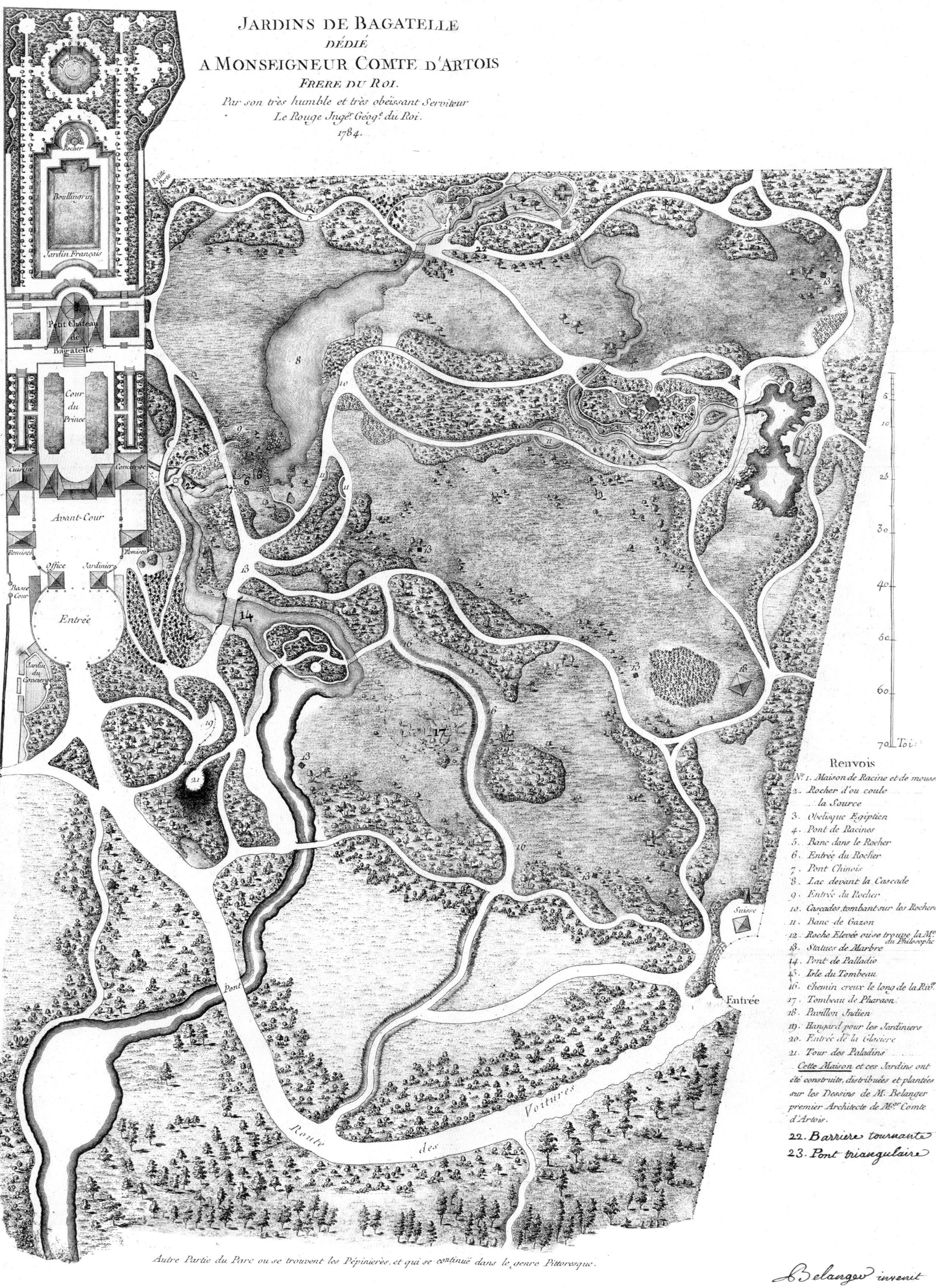
JARDINS DE BAGATELLE
DÉDIÉ
A MONSEIGNEUR COMTE D'ARTOIS
FRERE DU ROI.
Par son très humble et très obéissant Serviteur
Le Rouge Ingér. Géogr. du Roi.
1784.
Boullingrin
Rocher
Boullingrin
Jardin Français
Petit Chateau de Bagatelle
Cour du Prince
Cuisine
Concierge
Avant-Cour
Remises
Remises
Office
Jardinier
Basse Cour
Entrée
Jardin du Concierge
Pont
Suisse
Entrée
Route des Voitures
Renvois
N.° 1. Maison de Racine et de mousse
2. Rocher d'ou coule la Source
3. Obelisque Egiptien
4. Pont de Racines
5. Banc dans le Rocher
6. Entrée du Rocher
7. Pont Chinois
8. Lac devant la Cascade
9. Entrée du Rocher
10. Cascades tombant sur les Rochers
11. Banc de Gazon
12. Roche Elevée ou se trouve la Mon du Philosophe
13. Statues de Marbre
14. Pont de Palladio
15. Isle du Tombeau
16. Chemin creux le long de la Rivère
17. Tombeau de Pharaon.
18. Pavillon Indien
19. Hangard pour les Jardiniers
20. Entrée de la Glaciere
21. Tour des Paladins
Cette Maison et ces Jardins ont été construits, distribuées et plantées sur les Dessins de M. Belanger premier Architecte de Mgr. Comte d'Artois.
22. Barriere tournante
23. Pont triangulaire
70 Toi:
Autre Partie du Parc ou se trouvent les Pépinières, et qui se continuë dans le genre Pittoresque.
Belanger invenit

"Having, or even liking, such gardens is not enough—you need the eyes to see them and the legs to wander through them. I shall shortly lose use of both, given my old age and ailments. One of the last employments of my eyes was to read your most delightful book. I realize that I followed your precepts as far as my ignorance and fortune have allowed. I have everything on my grounds—flowerbeds, small pond, straight walks, very irregular woods, valleys, meadows, vineyard, and vegetable garden with shelter walls lined with fruit trees groomed and wild."

Letter from Voltaire to William Chambers,
August 7, 1772

Brown's new version of landscape never reigned in France, firstly because French taste remained strongly attached to the mid-century "Anglo-Chinois" model, but also because the spaces differed. Brown's art could express itself perfectly on the large estates of country homes in Britain, whereas French landscape gardens were often set in much smaller grounds closer to urban centers, as at Bagatelle and Monceau. You could not take a long horse ride through such grounds. People strolled on foot, organized parties there, and surprised guests with musicians or actors hidden in groves. The French-style landscape gardens remained "artificial playthings"[86] in total contrast to Brown's sprawling, patrician spaces, whose goal was to efface all traces of human activity, in a more rural spirit.

Bélanger, the comte d'Artois's architect, had visited many gardens during his trips to England, returning with numerous drawings of bridges and other follies. As in the realm of neo-Palladian architecture, Bélanger was heir to William Chambers, and he felt a garden should be a picturesque exercise in which artifices contributed to the creation of pictures.[87] A letter written to one of his clients, Madame Joly, illustrates this idea. In the following excerpt, Bélanger tries to convince her that the presence of a bridge is essential to the design of her garden, even if it spans no stream or river:

> Madame, I believe I must point out to you that a garden, being a life-size model of a landscape painting, should not be devoid of items (in this case, a bridge) that embellish the perspective of the picture, especially when they agree with decorum.... A garden cannot be created without a little poetry: hence, although not wanting too many follies, it should not be turned into a simple geographical map.... That is why, Madame, when responsible for a garden for a lady of taste, I felt I should not just draw winding paths at random, but must offer the eye the effect produced by the proposal, if executed, that I submitted to you through a landscape-design that I indicated above the plan.[88]

The grounds of Bagatelle were landscaped by Thomas Blaikie, a Scottish botanist and gardener who spent his entire career in France. It was the comte de Lauraguais who introduced Blaikie to Bélanger in 1777. Lauraguais had met Bélanger through the famous actress Sophie Arnould, whose lover he, too, had been up to 1769. The initial encounter between Blaikie and Bélanger was awkward. Initially amazed at the ignorance of the French, who asked him to design an English-style landscape garden for the château de Maisons, where the grounds were much too small, Blaikie finally agreed to work at Bagatelle, where he remained involved for over a decade. Despite difficulties—poor soil, lack of supplies, steady reductions in budget—a first version of the grounds was ready for a visit by the royal couple in 1780, and work accelerated again in 1782. The final result was a resounding success, although it is hard to tell whether that was due to Bélanger's talent or Blaikie's determined work. It might be supposed that the Scot concentrated on organizing perspectives and selecting plants, whereas the bridges and other follies were designed by the Frenchman. Bachaumont's memoirs offer an account of a visit there:

> One of the current destinations for an outing in the area around Paris is Bagatelle.... One does not see it upon arriving. One enters a little, uncultivated wood, which is merely surrounded by a simple fence. They are still working to make it more rustic, with rocks and sites whose dark, melancholy mood is enhanced. One arrives at the château only by a winding road. Finally there it is, and above it runs this motto: *Parva sed apta.* Six statues placed in the round entrance hall better typify its use: silence, mystery, folly, etc. Further on, Hercules with his finest attributes appears to share, with those statues, dominion over the premises. Everything is highly refined, down to the boundary markers and stones with their precious finish, or carving, or original color.[89]

PAGES 124–25
Louis-Gabriel Moreau, *The Obelisk and Waterfall on the Grounds of Bagatelle*, gouache, 1785 (private collection).

FACING PAGE
Overall View of the Grounds at Bagatelle, the Main Pavilion and Outbuildings, Built and Planted in 63 Days by Bélanger, Architect, Year 1782, engraving published in *Recueil d'Architecture Civile* by Jean-Charles Krafft, 1810. This plate includes picturesque views of the small Chinese bridge, the large wooden bridge, the big Chinese tent, and the philosopher's pavilion.

PAGES 128–29
Louis Bélanger, *View of the Pavilion and Grounds of Bagatelle*, gouache, 1785 (private collection).

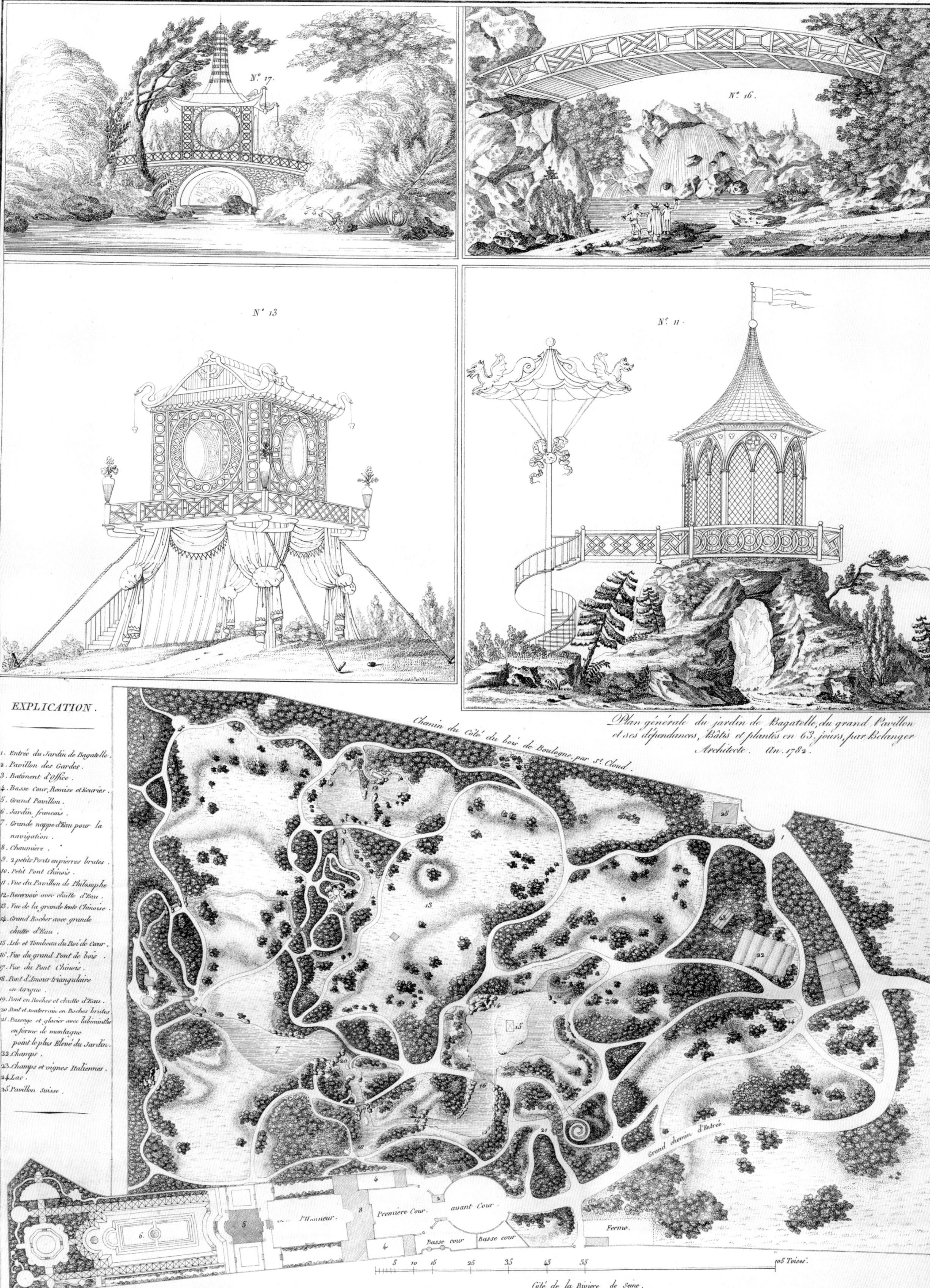

Krafft et Van lemcour Boullay et Gentot Sculp.

"May 29th. Messrs. Alban & Valet, directors of the manufactory in Javelle... have built an airship in their mill, christened Le Comte d'Artois. *They wished to dedicate their first efforts to the count, who authorized them to use his name. Upon learning that the duc d'Angoulême and the duc de Berry were at Bagatelle, they betook themselves there in their airship, and in the presence of those young princes and their court, navigated the airs as far as Longchamp, returning from Longchamp to Bagatelle. The comtesse d'Artois having gone to that same chateau at six o'clock in the evening, they recommenced the same maneuvers with still greater ease."*

Louis Petit de Bachaumont, *Mémoires Secrets*, May 29, 1785

ABOVE
Louis Chays, *Javel's Airship: The Comte d'Artois*, graphite, 1785 (Bibliothèque Nationale de France). In 1875, Léonard Alban and Mathieu Vallet, directors of the Compagnie de Javel, carried out a series of balloon flights. Filled with helium and endowed with the sails of a windmill, the balloon was christened *The Comte d'Artois*, after the company's patron. Adorned with the count's escutcheon, the balloon flew over Bagatelle on May 29, 1785, an event that made the English press.

ABOVE
François-Joseph Bélanger, *Design for a Wooden Bridge at Bagatelle*, pencil, ink, charcoal, and watercolor, c. 1785 (Drawing Matter Collection). The only known drawing in Bélanger's hand for the grounds of Bagatelle, this proposal shows the large wooden bridge and, on the right, the little Chinese bridge.

Priority was not given to the coherence or wholeness of the grounds, as it was in the architecture and interior decoration of Bagatelle, but rather to whimsy and changing experiences, also obtained through the great stylistic diversity of the follies.[90] Thanks to these constant changes of scene, the effect of surprise mentioned by Watkins was achieved. Thiéry's 1787 guidebook described a stroll through what the author called "the picturesque garden" at Bagatelle:

> Taking the first lane on the right, a few steps along one sees, on the left, a pavilion of the sort made by the Indians to shelter from wild beasts.... Continuing the promenade to the right, one comes to a rock from which springs the stream.... A bridge on the left, near a little island, leads to an enclosed grove, in the middle of which is an exposed rock supporting a Gothic pavilion called the Philosopher's House; it can be entered via a wonderfully light, spiral staircase shielded by a parasol. The balcony ringing this little building provides various views as interesting as they are pleasant.[91]

Everything was carefully arranged to delight the eye and stir the soul: plants, paths, streams, pavilions and, of course, the bridges so dear to Bélanger. Gouaches painted in 1785 by the architect's brother, Louis Bélanger, and Louis-Gabriel Moreau provide a striking impression of the grounds.[92] The gardens quickly became as famous as the Bagatelle Pavilion.

During the first festivities at Bagatelle in May 1780—the very day the famous wall came down with the wave of a magic wand—the queen joined her friends for a performance of the opera *Rose et Colas*.

> Queen Marie Antoinette played the role of the waiting maid, miladies de Polignac played the ingénue and the coquette; milord the comte d'Artois had to play the lead role.... When the long-anticipated day arrived, the cluster of carriages besieged Bagatelle and the comte d'Artois went forth to greet Their Majesties.
>
> Under a tent erected in the garden was an abundantly laden table; when everyone took their seat, it was noticed that several chairs were empty, notably the queen's. Just as concern was setting in, the back of the tent opened to reveal the tiers of a small theater, with velvet drapery for a curtain. Sedaine's comic opera was massacred by the actors, which did not prevent the audience from giving them a warm ovation. However, just as the queen finished one line, a whistle resounded.
>
> The stunned spectators looked at one another; but the queen, immediately realizing that only one among them could indulge in such insolence, moved to the front of the stage and said to the king: "Monsieur, since you are dissatisfied with my performance, please be so kind as to leave, your money will be reimbursed at the door." This heated exchange prompted applause, and the embarrassed king begged pardon for his brazenness from the queen as soon as she entered the ballroom, having changed out of her village-girl's costume. Despite this incident, the show ended rather well, and each went off satisfied.[93]

Blaikie described what happened next:

> This fete terminated with a ball in the Pavillon at which they all danced except the King who amuzed [*sic, passim*] in playing at Billiards at half a crown a game; at this rate he could never ruin his fortune; the whole terminated by illuminations all-round the Gardin. This day the King came from Lamuette to Bagatelle afoot; this fete was conducted with great Order and decorum with mirth; this was the first day that Bagatelle begane to make its apearance; this day I was presented to the King & Queen as Inspecteur of the counts Gardins who complimented me upon what I had already done.[94]

FACING PAGE
Élisabeth Vigée-Lebrun, *Marie Antoinette in a Park*, charcoal, stump, and white chalk on blue paper, c. 1780–81 (Metropolitan Museum of Art, New York). One of the few surviving drawings by Vigée-Lebrun, it shows the queen wearing a *robe à la polonaise* with its impressive volume of looped panels of fabric. The royal couple's first visit to Bagatelle took place during a party given by the comte d'Artois on May 20, 1780.

Despite the royal compliments, Blaikie was certainly annoyed by the constant damage done by these entertainments. After each party "the lawns and flowerbeds were trampled and shrubs were uprooted. The next morning the grounds were in the same state as if a barbarian army had camped there."[95] Gardening was a Sisyphean task, all the more discouraging given the apparent indifference of the owner, as revealed in another passage from Blaikie's diary penned in March 1783:

> As the Court resided at St Cloud which was bought by the Queen from the Duke of Orleans the Comte Dartois came and lodged at Bagatelle; this gave little disturbance to the place as he arrived frequently very late or rather in the morning from St Cloud and Generally hardly went out before he set off for Diner and seemed to take very little notice of anything, unless the melons which he took generally with him for the Queen.[96]

Blaikie then recounted a particularly revealing anecdote:

> However one day in the Morning arrived Mme de Polignac with some other ladys of honnour of the Queens to see Bagatelle and as the Comte was not up they desired not to call him; after walking and vewing the Gardens and asking me Many questions about the Comte and whether or not I was contented with him, I answered judiciously that I was not and that I never saw a more Lazier and a Man of less taste and that he had not once come to see the Gardens since he Lodged there.[97]

All this was reported to the queen, becoming the talk of the court, which found it highly amusing. Blaikie described his surprising encounter with the count the next morning:

> The Comte D'Artois came out and ... asked me "Well Blaikie are you not contented with me?" I told him no. "Why so?" "Because" says I "there is no pleasure in working for you as I hardly know whether or not I please you as you never come to see the works after so much expences and as I wish to please you and that you should enjoy my works." "What" says he "Is it only that? I promiss I will come and see you oftener." With that he took hold of my arm and walked all-round the Garden.[98]

The comte d'Artois was a peerless host at Bagatelle. Festivities and entertainments followed one another through the 1780s. Blaikie worked hard for the visit of the comte and comtesse du Nord (that is to say, Grand Duke Paul and Grand Duchess Maria of Russia) on June 1, 1782, as recounted by the baronne d'Oberkirch:

> In the morning I had been at Bagatelle with the comtesse du Nord. It is a charming little house in the Bois de Boulogne, belonging to the comte d'Artois who hosted us with his accustomed grace. We listened to a magnificent concert performed by the best musicians in Paris. The comtesse du Nord was enchanted. The refreshments served afterward were among the most stylish. There were the finest fresh fruits to be found anywhere. The comte d'Artois is the most pleasant prince in the world. He has a good mind, not in the style of the comte de Provence, that is to say serious and scholarly, but rather, a refined French wit, spirited and timely. The grand duchess was delighted. When it came time to leave, a courtier handed her the following impromptu, written in pencil:
>
> One scant approach shall I require
> to know you, worthy couple, right away.
> Should your true selves you wish to hide,
> then veil the virtues you clearly display.[99]

FACING PAGE
Detail of one of the ten statues punctuating the circular courtyard in front of the château de Bagatelle.

PAGES 138–39
John Hill, after John-Claude Nattes, *View of the Landscape Garden at Bagatelle, Near Paris, Bridge at Bagatelle*, aquatint published in *Versailles, Paris and Saint Denis*, 1809. This etching of the large wooden bridge connecting two huge rocks is a thoroughly Romantic vision of sublime, grandiose nature.

*"Bagatelle is an enchanting spot.
The pretty pavilion that acts as château
is surrounded by a perfectly designed
landscape garden. It includes a stream
fed by a fire pump... with many bridges
over the stream, arbors, thatched huts,
in short, everything imaginable of
this sort. The grounds are maintained
with exquisite refinement."*

Mémoires de la baronne d'Oberkirch, June 15, 1784

We do not know whether this missive was followed by an invitation to return to Bagatelle, incognito, to take better advantage of its hidden charms. As the years went by, Blaikie continued to work on the gardens despite the looming threats and troubles that were wracking the kingdom. The reputation of the comte d'Artois continued to deteriorate. In 1781 the superintendent of his household, Radix de Sainte-Foy, was removed from his office and tried for embezzlement.[100] The corrupt, incompetent Sainte-Foy was largely responsible for the poor management and spectacular debts incurred by the count's household. Once he was dismissed, an end was put to the most extravagant expenditures, such as the rebuilding of the château de Saint-Germain and the château de Maisons. But neither Artois's behavior nor his image improved. By 1789 his qualities of friendliness and refined wit were no longer being mentioned. He was criticized for being a frivolous spendthrift and for corrupting the court and queen, for sticking to the "Polignac clique," and for advocating a hard line towards the Third Estate. Madame Campan lamented as much in her diary as the Revolution got underway:

> The people nevertheless still spoke of the king with fondness ... but they believed his thinking was rigid, due to the opinions and influence of the comte d'Artois and the Queen, and those two august people were then the target of hate by the discontented.... The people's fury was aimed at the comte d'Artois, whose unfavorable opinion on the double representation [of the Third Estate] appeared to be a heinous crime. Several times they shouted at him, "God save the king, despite you, Sir, and your opinions!"

In a revealing anecdote, when an angry crowd later broke into the château de Versailles, one better disposed woman gave Madame Campan's sister (who, like her, was a lady-in-waiting to the queen), this wise piece of advice: "Above all, remove ... that sash of green ribbon—'tis the sash of that Artois, whom we will never forgive."[101]

Just a few days after the Bastille fell, Bagatelle was threatened. Blaikie just managed to escaped the people's wrath. "In returning by the Barrières de Roulle there was hundreds perhaps thousands of people assembled, some crying out to go to Bagatelle to Burn it, as the Comte d'Artois seemed at the time to be the person the Most detested."[102] The courageous gardener still managed to reach the château:

> The porter Polonais had left the gate so that at last I found my old servant Lafrance who was hid amongst the trees and when he heard the horse called to me and told me as they had heard that they were coming to burn Bagatelle and probably misacre [*sic, passim*] the people that everyone had fled and that as he expected I should probably arrive and not know he waited for me; we agreed not to unsadle the horse but to keep in readyness in case of an attack.[103]

Miraculously, the estate escaped destruction and fire. By 1790 the count had long fled abroad, but Blaikie was still there. Aware that a chapter—indeed, an entire era—had come to a close, Blaikie reported his touching farewell to Marie Antoinette:

> One day Mme Elizabeth came and walked in the garden and amongst some Conversation about the Revolution I told her what I thought and that they had to do with a bad set of People who wished to Sacrifice them and many other things which

PAGE 140
The large water-lily pond features aquatic plants.

FACING PAGE
Jean-Antoine Watteau, *Voulez-vous Triompher des Belles?* (Would You Like to Win Over the Ladies?), oil on canvas, c. 1714–17 (Wallace Collection, London). This flirtatious little painting was bought in 1848 by Lord Henry Seymour, brother of the marquess of Hertford, who owned Bagatelle in the nineteenth century. In 1853 it went to Seymour's nephew, Richard Wallace.

> surprized her; after coming and resting herself in my house which she admired for its cleanlyness she returned to Paris and told the King and Queen what I had Said, so that some days afterwards the Queen came and enquired of the Porter where I was.... So I soon joined her who told her Suitte that She did not want them as she was with me and would see the Garden; she told me "You had a Visite from My Sister Elizabeth who told me what you said. I know your way of thinking and shall never forget you."[104]

The woman who would never forget died on the scaffold on October 16, 1793, whereas Blaikie made it through the succeeding regimes up to the July Monarchy of the 1830s. During the Empire period, he notably worked for Empress Joséphine on her estate at Malmaison. When the Bourbon monarchy was restored in 1814, the comte d'Artois returned to France—but not to Bagatelle. His country retreat would meet with a different fate.

And yet the interior decoration, the gardens, and, above all, Bélanger's masterful architecture would remain a reference for decades. The remarkable persistence of its influence is illustrated by the reaction of the famous German architect Friedrich Gilly and his pupil, Karl Friedrich Schinkel.[105] Gilly visited Bagatelle in 1797 and wrote an enthusiastic essay for his father's publication, *Essays on Architecture* (see the opening of chapter 3).[106] He designed a copy, Möltersche Haus, for the Tiergarten in Berlin, which became one of the most famous country houses, or *Landhaüser*, in the Germanic states.

Bagatelle also featured prominently in Gilly's teachings, whose impact was crucial to the career and work of Schinkel, himself the father of German neoclassical architecture in the nineteenth century. "Schinkel's admired mentors, Friedrich and David Gilly, both inducted their pupils into a hands-on relationship with building, first by means of copying instructive examples, and then by assisting on construction sites. One of the staples of this training was the château de Bagatelle in Paris, in the Bois de Boulogne."[107] It is easy to imagine Friedrich Gilly with his pupils, taking up the essay he wrote in 1799:

> The celerity with which this project was set in hand and the method employed entitle it to be considered something of an architectural miracle.... The exterior, every detail of which is executed with great care and precision, has the natural color of the ashlar blocks of which the building is composed. Its pale-yellow hue, mellowed by weathering, lends the building, in common with the majority of those in Paris, an extremely pleasing appearance.[108]

Following this admiring description, the professor concluded:

> This taste, applied with sensitive discrimination throughout and coupled with an equal perfection of workmanship, delights the eye at every turn and adds the utmost charm to the character of the building.... With this project, Mr. Bélanger firmly establishes the reputation that he now properly enjoys. He is one of the few artists to have given an entirely new direction to French architecture and will undoubtedly raise it to the heights of perfection.[109]

The stage was set for history to play its role.

FACING PAGE
Alexandre Moitte, *Madame Élisabeth Embracing Marie Antoinette*, black chalk (Palais des Beaux-Arts, Lille). The affectionate melancholy of this scene is reminiscent of the two women's respective farewells to the gardener Thomas Blaikie during their last visits to the grounds of Bagatelle in 1790.

PAGES 146–47
The south-facing entrance to Bagatelle is preceded by a sunken courtyard set between two gritstone terraces.

Chapter 5

Revolution, Empire, Restoration

Bagatelle as Imperial and Princely Residence

"June 21st—the duc de Berry treated me to a hunt in the Bois de Boulogne and dinner with the royal family and the entire court at Bagatelle. The day was charming. I greatly enjoyed myself."

Maria Carolina, duchesse de Berry, 1816

In his 1820 memoirs of the duc de Berry, Chateaubriand included the following anecdote:

> Humanity is a follower of charity, or rather a component part of it.... [The king's brother] had presented to his young son the cottage of Bagatelle, of which so much was said at the time of the Revolution, though one of Bonaparte's undercommissaries would have disdained [its gardens and furnishings]. The duc de Berry was very fond of this little rural retreat, and his bounty supported all the poor in its neighborhood. In the summer season he frequently went there very early in the morning. On one occasion, on his way through the Bois de Boulogne, he met a child heavily laden with a large basket. The prince stopped his cabriolet. "Where are you going, my little fellow?" said he. "To carry this basket to Muette," answered the child. "It is too heavy for you," said the duke, "give it [to] me, and I will deliver it on my way by." The basket was taken into the cabriolet, and faithfully delivered. The duke then sought out the child's father, and said to him, "I met your little boy; you make him carry loads too heavy for him, and will thereby injure his health, and check his growth; buy an ass to carry the basket for him." And he gave money for the purchase.
>
> When great monarchs, or very celebrated persons, choose to mix in disguise with the people, curiosity delights to seek them out, and discover their actions. No virtues are, however, more easy to practice than those called into action on such occasions. Human pride soars the higher from such self-abasement. Those striking circumstances of strong contrast are not to be met with in the life of the duc de Berry. He was not a king; he did not yet possess that celebrity death was so soon to confer on him. Accustomed to obscurity, it was nothing new to him to mix with the inferior orders of society. It was then the superiority of his own nature which gave an indescribable charm to all his words and actions. The man was loved and admired in the prince, even before that scene which was to make him perfectly known.[110]

The comte d'Artois's excessive lavishness, festivities, endless nights of gambling, and dissoluteness seem far away. Praise was given to good morals, closeness to the people, simplicity, and charity. The ancien régime was no more. Through Revolution, Empire, and Restoration, France was entering the nineteenth century.

The château de Bagatelle miraculously survived all those vicissitudes, and still belonged to the Bourbon family. The duc de Berry, son of the comte d'Artois and Maria Theresa of Savoy, was born on January 24, 1778, just a few months after the famous bet with Marie Antoinette. He was assassinated in 1820 while leaving the opera house. It was the duke's tragic fate that prompted Chateaubriand to write a memoir of him.

But how did we get to this point? During the Revolution, Bagatelle was first confiscated by the new government, then sold and turned into a venue for public entertainment during the Directory period, only to be bought by Napoleon, and finally handed back to the comte d'Artois, who gave it to his son, the duc de Berry.

Having left France at the outbreak of the Revolution, the comte d'Artois was apparently able to safely store some of the château's furnishings, but the building itself soon suffered the same fate as all Crown property. In the new administration system, the Boulogne side of the wall enclosing

PAGE 149
Detail of the clock on the guard house at the entrance.

FACING PAGE
Nicolas Marie Joseph Chapuy, after Antoine-Pierre Mongin, *The Château and Part of the Grounds of Bagatelle*, acquaint, early nineteenth century (Musée Carnavalet – Histoire de Paris, Paris).

Bagatelle became the border between the municipalities of Neuilly and Boulogne-lez-Paris; the estate itself thus became part of Neuilly, which had charge of it. Whereas the château de La Muette and the château de Madrid were sold and demolished in 1793, Bagatelle was spared once again, although permanently emptied of its furnishings and paintings (except those by Hubert Robert and Callet, in very poor condition). In 1797, the Directory put the property up for sale, and it was bought by a Paris entrepreneur who turned it into a music and dance hall. Parties were held there, and Bagatelle became a favorite destination for Parisian outings and fashionable gatherings, as it was already announced by this verse dedicated to Sophie Arnould during the construction of the castle:

Si vous voulez vous promener *Dans ce bois, charmante Isabelle,* *Nous pourrions, sans nous détourner,* *Aller jusqu'à Bagatelle.* ... *Quoi ! déjà votre pied mignon* *Dans ces sables tourne et chancelle,* *Asseyons-nous sur ce gazon ;* *C'est le chemin de Bagatelle...*[111]	If in these woods you fain would stroll, my charming Isabelle, let's head straight down that long, fair lane, as far as Bagatelle. ... What, already in this sand your ankle fair doth twist and swell? Then let us sit upon this lawn, 'Tis on the path to Bagatelle.

This interlude of fun and games did not last long. The Directory was followed by the Consulate, then by the Empire. Napoleon regularly went hunting at Saint-Cloud, at Versailles, in the forest of Saint-Germain, and at Bagatelle. He finally bought the latter property in 1806 and began restoring it in 1809 when Pierre Fontaine, first architect to the emperor, got down to work: "The Emperor returned to Saint-Cloud yesterday. I received the order to take up the plans for the pavilion of Bagatelle.... I must restore that little house as soon as the estimates of expenditure have been approved." A little later, Fontaine reported: "I presented an estimate of the expenditures on the pavilion of Bagatelle amounting to 160,000 francs, and the Emperor accorded the credits in order to get this house in a usable condition, as promptly as possible, for hunting parties and summer suppers."[112]

The poor condition of the building required major renovation, and the interior paintings were largely redone. As the duc de Frioul—"Napoleon's shadow"—reported in March 1811, "Today H[is] M[ajesty] went to dine at the pavilion of Bagatelle; he did me the honor of telling me he wished to take advantage of the summer months to restore the interior paintings, which are not fresh and not to his liking." In August of that same year, the duke added, "His Majesty would like to give Bagatelle the name of Pavillon de Hollande, and wants that name to be inscribed there as was done for the Pavillon d'Italie at Saint-Cloud."[113]

In addition to renovations, a complete refurnishing was necessary. It was decided to use some of the furniture bought for Élisa Bonaparte's private mansion. Having become grand duchess of Tuscany, she had moved to the Palazzo Pitti in Florence. "I am pleased to inform you, Sir, that building work on the arrangement of the pavilion of Bagatelle is completed, and that His Majesty will use it as a hunting lodge during his next stay in Paris. It must be furnished. His Majesty has approved the use, to this end, of some of the furniture bought for the residence of H[er] I[mperial] H[ighness] the Grand Duchess of Tuscany, which has since been stored in the Imperial Wardrobe."[114]

FACING PAGE
Cross-section of the Pavilion Taken from the Middle, engraving published in *Recueil d'Architecture Civile* by Jean-Charles Krafft, 1810 (collection of the author).

Coupe du Pavillon prise au milieu.

ABOVE
Plan of the Grounds of Bagatelle Measured by Mr Boucher and Drawn by Captain Nicolas of the Royal Corps of Geographical Engineers in 1814, watercolor, 1814 (Musée Carnavalet – Histoire de Paris, Paris).

Nord
Chemin de Boulogne a Neuilly
Cour du Manège
Première Cour
Cour d'Honneur
Partie du Jardin de Madrid
le Colimaçon
Regard
Porte d'entrée
la Reine Marguerite
DE BOULOGNE

The comte d'Artois's pavilion was thus repaired, restored, refurnished, and renamed. Bagatelle would henceforth perform a new role: as a hunting lodge, it symbolized the exercise of imperial government, and as the residence of Napoleon's infant son, styled the king of Rome, it embodied dynastic continuity. (Bagatelle would later play this same double role during the Bourbon Restoration.)

Napoleon's re-establishment of royal hunts during the imperial era was first of all a way for him to symbolically confirm his control of the state apparatus, even as it perpetuated the heritage of earlier regimes. Hunts on horseback for deer, or outings to shoot wild game, were held on other former royal estates as well as Bagatelle. The emperor particularly liked to shoot, and Empress Marie-Louise often joined him, after which the imperial couple would dine together at the comte d'Artois's old table.[115] An article in the *Mercure de France* dated December 1, 1810, reported on the military "capture," so to speak, of Bagatelle:

> At this time major restorations are being carried out on the pavilion of Bagatelle, now an imperial property designed to serve as a hunting lodge. Built in 1780, this little house was a masterpiece of refinement and elegance—over the door was an inscription that described its scale and its purpose. The boudoir, decorated with paintings by Greuze, Fragonard, and Lagrenée, was however more remarkable for its lavish décor than for its art. It is hard to fathom why the architect decided to give the bedroom of the prince—the former owner of these delightful premises—the form of a tent, filling it with military attributes so unsuited to the time, place, and person.... The outbuildings, completely detached from the main house, indicate the care taken to hide from prying eyes the mysterious scenes played out in this charming theater.[116]

By one of those twists of history, the emperor, a true military leader, became a more worthy occupant of Bagatelle than its pleasure-loving creator.

Once his heir, the king of Rome, was born on March 20, 1811, Napoleon envisaged the construction of an immense palace for his son on the hill of Chaillot. The project, assigned to Fontaine and his partner, Charles Percier, was to be at the center of a military and administrative city representing the "largest and most extraordinary construction of the century." The colossal plan included the place de l'Étoile, the Bois de Boulogne, La Muette, and Bagatelle, covering a surface area equal to the entire city of Paris at that time.[117] In a wistful tone, Fontaine described the views one would have had from the palace:

> At sunset, from the other side, the Seine presented a no less magnificent, and much more delightful, picture as it flowed away from Paris. Again seen in its various meanders, the river would snake between the lush slopes of Sèvres, Meudon, and Saint-Cloud, which filled the horizon on that side....
>
> Over by Passy, the château de La Muette, as headquarters of the hunt, would have led to a pheasant farm and to a vast menagerie which, housing a large number of rare animals of all kinds,... would have been extended the entire width of the Bois de Boulogne as far as the high road of Neuilly, near the gate of Maillot.

FACING PAGE
Carle Vernet, *Napoleon I Hunting in the Bois de Boulogne* (detail), oil on canvas, 1811 (Hermitage Museum, Saint Petersburg). Although not a good huntsman, Napoleon wanted to follow royal tradition by reinstating official hunts as early as 1802. In addition to the forests of Compiègne and Fontainebleau, he would hunt in the Bois de Boulogne, when the day might end with a private dinner at Bagatelle with Empress Marie-Louise.

> The little Bagatelle pavilion was to be used as a hunting lodge at the edge of the woods, near the banks of the Seine which, after a long detour, would complete the enclosure of the grounds since, in order to enlarge them further, all the lands on the plain between the woods and the river were to be bought and planted.[118]

The Empire's first military setbacks and the catastrophic Russian campaign put an end to that grandiose project, doomed to remain an architect's dream. Bagatelle continued to be a simple country retreat for the imperial family, where they could spend a few restful days far from the bustle of the world. Fontaine described one of those days, February 22, 1812. The pleasure of returning to Bagatelle was tinged with regret for former ambitions:

> The emperor, while hunting in the Bois de Boulogne, went to Bagatelle. He visited the house and went over part of the grounds. The furnishing and decoration of the rooms, and the general state of things, all seemed very good to him. He asked that everything be kept with the greatest care so that the king of Rome could stay there for several days. Then, strolling through the lanes of the gardens, he asked me about the neighboring properties, and his earlier plans to buy all the land between the grounds and the Seine, as far as Neuilly.[119]

Bagatelle, like other imperial residences, served as a stage for the dynastic link between Napoleon and his son. From 1812 onward, that continuity was increasingly underscored, notably in paintings with titles such as *Napoleon at Lunch Playing with the King of Rome, Empress Marie-Louise Guiding the King of Rome's First Steps*, and so on. The "Pavillon de Hollande" became one of those private spots where Napoleon could be presented as a good father rather than an "ogre." The figure of the imperial child, meanwhile, represented the promise of the future.[120]

Obtaining this much-desired heir called for an enormous sacrifice on the part of Joséphine. The new empress, Marie-Louise, archduchess of Austria, mother of the king of Rome, did not want her son presented to Joséphine. But at the latter's insistence, Napoleon finally agreed to organize a secret meeting in 1812. The scene took place at Bagatelle, and was witnessed by Napoleon's first groom of the chamber, Constant:

> One day, Madame de Montesquiou received an order from Napoleon to take the little king to Bagatelle. [Joséphine] had obtained the favor of seeing the child whose birth had sparked celebrations in Europe.... The royal child was presented to her. I know nothing in the world so touching as the joy of that excellent woman upon seeing Napoleon's son. She first gazed upon him with fearful eyes, then took him in her arms, pressing him to her breast with indescribable tenderness.... The interview was brief, yet how full it had been! It was then that the sincerity of her sacrifice could be judged by her joy.[121]

Joséphine made the ultimate sacrifice, but to what end? Fontaine, who kept his position after Napoleon fell, recounted what happened next in his diary.[122] "The Office of Royal Works now finds itself deprived of several houses that were returned to the families of those people who had previously owned them. Bagatelle and the Roules stables were returned to the comte d'Artois, and M. Bélanger, who built them both, took possession in the count's name."[123]

FACING PAGE
Pierre-François-Léonard Fontaine, *Project for the Palace of the King of Rome* (detail), watercolor and wash, 1811 (École Nationale Supérieure des Beaux-Arts, Paris). When the King of Rome was born in 1811, Napoleon ordered the construction of a huge palace on the hill of Chaillot to glorify his heir. The colossal project included the Bois de Boulogne, the château de La Muette, and Bagatelle. It remained an architect's dream.

The Empire was no more. Bagatelle witnessed the departure of Napoleon, the empress, and their child. They were succeeded by the duc and duchesse de Berry, then by the duke's daughter and son. (That son, styled, duc de Bordeaux, was the "miracle child" and later a tragic actor in French history when known as the comte de Chambord, alias "Henry V the pretender.")

After an initial restoration, followed by Napoleon's return to power for "one hundred days," the Bourbons permanently recovered the throne. But the situation was fragile, and the court was a veritable wasps' nest. It included the two surviving grandsons of Louis XV, that is, Louis XVI's brothers: the comte de Provence, who became King Louis XVIII, and the comte d'Artois, henceforth "Monsieur," as brother to the king. The count's eldest son, Louis Antoine, duc d'Angoulême, married the daughter of Louis XVI and Marie Antoinette, Marie-Thérèse, "Madame Royale." She never got over the trauma of the Revolution, of the imprisonment and execution of her father and mother. Henceforth called the duchesse d'Angoulême, she was the ghost of the ancien régime. Alone, she often visited the Chapelle Expiatoire consecrated in 1824 to the memory of her parents, built from the very materials that were initially gathered for Napoleon's planned imperial palace on the hill of Chaillot.[124]

The Angoulême couple had no children and hopes for an heir shifted to the comte d'Artois's younger son, the duc de Berry, and his wife, Maria Carolina of Bourbon-Two Sicilies. Their marriage had to not just ensure the continuity of the French branch of the Bourbons but also bring a glow of the future and the sparkle of youth to the court. Maria Carolina descended from the Spanish branch of the Bourbons, that is to say Phillip V of Spain, the grandson of Louis XIV. She would become one of the more romantic and flamboyant figures in the history of nineteenth-century France. She was the granddaughter of Francis I, king of Naples, who became King Ferdinand I of Two Sicilies, and Maria Carolina of Austria, the sister of Marie Antoinette. Unlike her many cousins, little Maria Carolina was not brought up in the strict atmosphere of a European court. She grew up at the gateway to Africa, in the shade and light of Sicily, in a fanciful court with a hint of the Far East. This would permanently shape her character.[125]

The choice of Maria Carolina as a bride seems shrewd. Her freshness, energy, and character rejuvenated the court and delighted the people of Paris. The Sicilian princess's love of dancing and festivities brought new life to the Tuileries Palace. Despite the groom's numerous infidelities, the Berry couple was a happy one. After two miscarriages, the duchess gave birth to a girl, Louise, in 1819. The future looked bright.

As Fontaine already mentioned, the comte d'Artois had recovered possession of Bagatelle, but preferred to pass it on to his younger son. The count probably wanted to forget his youthful antics. His character had changed following the cataclysm of the Revolution, and ever since he had met Madame de Polastron. His excessive taste in luxury had given way to a return to the Catholic faith, and an obsession with restoring the ancien régime. It is hard to reconcile the young, spirited prince who had fun with Marie Antoinette, with the man who would later become the austere, devout, thoroughly conservative King Charles X.

PAGES 160–61
Pierre Courvoisier, *Bagatelle Seen from the South Entrance*, watercolor, c. 1815–20 (Musée Carnavalet – Histoire de Paris, Paris).

FACING PAGE
François Gérard, *The Duchesse de Berry in the Park of Bagatelle*, oil on canvas (Amsterdam, Rijksmuseum). Marie Caroline of Bourbon, princess of the Two Sicilies, married the duc de Berry in 1816. Her youthfulness, gaiety, and penchant for entertainment lit up the French court. Here she poses in the grounds of Bagatelle, where her children grew up.

The new owner of Bagatelle, the duc de Berry, made it the headquarters of his hunts,[126] a symbol of the restored monarchy. The first outings took place in July 1814, just months after the Empire first collapsed:

> The duc de Berry hunted deer yesterday in the Bois de Boulogne. The party was large and brilliant. Many women went in carriages to enjoy the sight. Once the stag was run down in their presence, His Royal Highness invited them all ... to take some refreshments under a tent set up in Bagatelle.... Thus the grace and goodness of French princes have restored to us the good old days of French gaiety, manners, and urbanity.[127]

Hunting was a show, a demonstration, striking proof that royalty was back—and also, paradoxically, that one regime followed in the footsteps of another. On August 24, 1814, a new outing was organized, this time followed by a splendid ball widely reported in the press.

Early in March 1815, when news reached Paris that Napoleon had escaped from Elba in order to return to power, a hunt was held at Bagatelle. The fallen emperor's arrival in France sparked widespread disbelief. As the duchesse de Gontaut reported, "The news was taken to be absurd madness, which I found it all the harder to believe in that I had just received a letter from the duc de Berry recounting a party he had given, beginning with a hunt in the Bois de Boulogne, and then a luncheon supper and little ball at his pretty house of Bagatelle; some of my family had attended and he was so kind as to say I was the only one missing."[128]

Berry didn't believe the emperor could return, and he snidely informed his guests of "an unexpected visit." In an irony of history, one month later, on April 1, 1815, Napoleon entered Bagatelle as a conqueror.[129] His return lasted a mere one hundred days, but the humiliation left a deep mark on the Bourbons.

The affront was only redressed by a highly symbolic event reported in the *Journal des Débats* on January 22, 1817:

> Saturday last, H.R.H the duc de Berry took pleasure in hunting in the forest of Fontainebleau.... His Royal Highness noticed a bird of immense size soaring at a great height above his head. The prince grabbed a loaded gun carried by one of his officers, took aim at the bird and shattered its wing, bringing it down at his feet. It was an eagle of the most powerful species, and, being merely wounded, struggled long and hard against those who would seize it. They were obliged to kill the eagle to overcome it. It was taken to the museum of natural history, where it is to be stuffed.[130]

At last: a symbol of the ultimate victory over Napoleon. Artist Charles Louis François Quinart immortalized the incident in a painting exhibited at the Salon of 1819. Meanwhile, the eagle had been given to a taxidermist and was displayed at Bagatelle alongside the painting. Artois's former country retreat thus became the metaphorical cradle of revenge, of regal power reconquered at the barrel of a gun.[131]

Yet the bird proved to be a bad omen. Fate was unrelenting, and it was cruel. Just a few years later, on the night of February 13–14, 1820, as he was leaving the opera house, the duc de Berry himself was brought down by Louis Pierre Louvel, a Bonapartist laborer who said he wanted to "wipe out the Bourbon roots." This was the revenge of "the Eagle," a disaster for the Royalist party, and a catastrophe for the duchesse de Berry.

FACING PAGE
Sèvres Porcelain Manufactory, *Bagatelle Pavilion Seen from the Entrance*, a plate from the "Various Views" service, painted by François Davignon, 1816 (Mobilier National, on indefinite loan to the château de Fontainebleau).

"Today the duc de Berry gave a charming party at Bagatelle, after a hunt in the Bois de Boulogne followed by many riders and carriages filled with elegant women. They gathered in the pavilion. Tents had been set up in the grounds of Bagatelle, and tables elegantly provisioned. After the banquet, the guests danced; a lively joy lit up this fair party."

Journal des Débats, August 25, 1814

PAGE 167
François Gérard, *Charles Ferdinand d'Artois, Duc de Berry, in Hunting Dress*, oil on panel, c. 1820 (Châteaux de Versailles et de Trianon, Versailles). When the monarchy was restored and the comte d'Artois became King Charles X, he abandoned Bagatelle, leaving the estate to his younger son, the duc de Berry, who made it his hunting lodge as early as July 1814.

LEFT
Charles Louis François Quinart and Hippolyte Lecomte, *Charles Ferdinand d'Artois, Duc de Berry, Shooting an Eagle in the Forest of Fontainebleau*, oil on canvas, 1818 (Wimpole Hall, Cambridgeshire). Exhibited at the Salon of 1819, this painting was later hung at Bagatelle alongside a stuffed eagle—the symbol of Napoleon—that had been brought down by the duke himself.

Henceforth a widow, Maria Carolina became the new mistress of Bagatelle. She had already had an opportunity to appreciate the little château and grounds built by her father-in-law. The very day after her wedding, the duchess wrote:

> June 18th—I went to dine with the King and family, and then heard Mass, after which I received ambassadors, foreign ministers, and their wives. Then I went for a stroll at my husband's pretty little country house, called Bagatelle. I dined at the Tuileries [Palace], which I will do every day, and afterward I returned to the charming Elysée-Bourbon palace, where we live.[132]

Four days after the marriage, the entire court went to Bagatelle to continue the celebrations. Thus life went on, happily, until that fateful day in February 1820, when suddenly everything changed.

The devoutly desired heir would nevertheless appear, because the duchess was pregnant when her husband was assassinated. On September 29, 1820, seven and a half months after the tragic incident at the opera, she gave birth to a son, Henri, the "miracle child," the descendent of the Bourbon dynasty that the assassin sought to eradicate. The kingdom was jubilant!

The young mother was immensely proud of having produced an heir to the throne, but her joy was mixed. The upbringing of her little Henri, heir presumptive, would become an affair of state, beyond her control. Henri and his sister were raised by their governess, the duchesse de Gontaut, and then by the young prince's governor, the baron de Damas.

Maria Carolina suffered from the heavy, lugubrious atmosphere of the palaces of the Tuileries and Saint-Cloud. To escape these haunts of ghosts, she often went to the château de Rosny, purchased in 1818, but this removed her even further from her children, who grew up alone in the shade of the trees planted by their grandfather.

Built by a young prince who was never expected to reign, designed for fun and parties, the "pleasure house" evolved into a children's playground where the unexpected grandchild of a no less improbable king would spend his early years. As early as May 1820, the duchesse de Gontaut dispatched Madame Bayart, the wet-nurse she had just recruited in anticipation of the newborn child, to Bagatelle with very clear instructions. "Do not over-tire yourself. Write to me as soon as you set out. At Bagatelle you will be very well cared for, and I will spend three hours there every morning with Mademoiselle. I will thus be able to see you often, to ensure that you are happy and well.... The milk of someone as virtuous as yourself has been sent to us by Providence for this child destined for the finest throne in the world."[133]

So little Henri and his sister grew up at Bagatelle, where they received visits from their mother, although their everyday lives were spent with their governor and governess.

> After the birth of Mademoiselle and the duc de Bordeaux, this miniature château with its charming, shady grounds became the usual promenade of the Royal Children of France. Often there were refreshments, games, and entertainments of all kinds to which the two princely children invited others of their age.... At the recent Universal Exposition there appeared the elegant, curious carriage in which they take the duc de Bordeaux out for strolls, to which two tame, docile white sheep were harnessed. It was a small, eight-spring calash lined in white and upholstered in green, the colors of Artois.[134]

FACING PAGE
Louis Hersent, *Henri-Charles-Ferdinand d'Artois and his Sister, Louise-Marie-Thérèse d'Artois*, oil on canvas, 1821 (Châteaux de Versailles et de Trianon, Versailles). Henri-Charles-Ferdinand d'Artois, duc de Bordeaux, was born seven and a half months after the assassination of his father, the duc de Berry. He and his elder sister, styled Mademoiselle d'Artois, grew up at Bagatelle.

PAGES 172–73
François-Edme Ricois, *The Family of Charles-Ferdinand, Duc de Berry, in the Grounds of the Château of Bagatelle*, oil on canvas, 1825 (Royal Collection Trust, London). Under the Bourbon Restoration, the comte d'Artois's pleasure house became the playground of the royal children. They were raised there by a governess, the duchesse de Gontaut, followed by the young prince's tutor, baron de Damas.

Meanwhile, Fontaine wrote in his diary that, "The duchesse de Berry, after the somber death of her husband, continued to stroll through Bagatelle in fine weather, and every day Madame de Gontaut, governess of the Royal Children, takes her pupils there to allow them to recover from the fatigues of education. Baron de Damas, the young duc de Bordeaux's governor, now shares sovereignty over the premises with the governess."[135]

What about the château itself? Had it been restored? Were the furnishings and decoration revamped by the new occupants? Unlike Maria Carolina, who had little background in the arts, the duc de Berry was a connoisseur. As Vigée-Lebrun later recounted from London in her memoirs, "The son of [the comte d'Artois], M. le duc de Berri, often called to see me in the mornings. Sometimes he would arrive carrying a small bundle of paintings which he had picked up for a very reasonable price. This proved how knowledgeable he was on the subject of painting: they were superb examples of Wouvermans, yet it needed a fine eye indeed to appreciate the beauty that lay underneath the layers of dirt. I have seen ... these painting since in his home, the Élysée-Bourbon Palace."[136] For that matter, as collector and patron, the duc de Berry bought fifteen paintings at the Salon of 1814, including two by Boilly and various genre subjects that he had delivered to Bagatelle straightaway.[137]

Once she was with the duke and his entourage, Maria Carolina learned quickly, soon imposing her taste at court. But that was not yet the case when she married in 1816. On moving into the Elysée-Bourbon Palace, the couple retained most of the furnishings and decoration installed by Napoleon's sister and, later, by Marie-Louise, apparently from a combination of shared taste and a concern to limit expenditure. Louis XVIII's court thus lived in an Empire environment, with mahogany furniture everywhere!

It was only toward the end of the decade, after the château de Rosny was bought, followed by her move to the Marsan pavilion of the Louvre when she became a widow, that Maria Carolina steadily emancipated herself from the style associated with the Royal Wardrobe and the conservatism of the court. She first favored furniture in pale, "indigenous" woods, then fell for the "Gothic" fashion. She was a great reader of Sir Walter Scott and sympathetic to the avant-gardes, even becoming a ring-leader of Romanticism and the French Gothic revival or *troubadour* movement.[138]

The duc and duchesse de Berry seem to have made few changes to the Empire decoration of Bagatelle. The archives mention maintenance work, the replacement of carpets and similar expenditures, but no major transformations. The refurnishing, which only took place after Napoleon's Hundred Days, was apparently fairly modest and retained the dominant "mahogany" style.[139] Some of the major decorative features installed under the comte d'Artois, such as Bélanger's ceilings, remained in place throughout the Restoration period.[140] The tastes of the duke and duchess found expression elsewhere. The large orders placed with Jacob-Desmalter for Gothic furnishings were destined for the Marsan pavilion, while it was the château de Rosny that received the duchess's attention, notably via countless purchases of furniture, objects, paintings, and books.

Suppliers' invoices provide testimony to the evolution of Bagatelle. Up to 1820, they were addressed to "His Royal Highness the duc de Berry," then in 1820–21 to "Her Royal Highness the duchesse de Berry," followed in 1822 by "Their Royal Highnesses the Children of France" or "His Royal Highness the duc de Bordeaux." Large purchases of toys were further proof that Bagatelle had been passed on to the children.[141]

FACING PAGE
Alexandre-Jean Dubois-Drahonnet, *Portrait of the Duchesse de Berry*, oil on canvas, 1828 (Musée de Picardie, Amiens). The duchesse de Berry was a great reader of Sir Walter Scott as well as a muse of Romanticism and the Gothic revival. Here she poses in the Tuileries Palace in dress that expresses her trend-setting taste: her fur-trimmed velvet gown is cinched with a large "Gothic" belt supplied by Fossin the jeweler.

The upbringing of the two children was closely monitored by their grandfather, the king (the comte d'Artois having become Charles X on the death of his brother, Louis XVIII), and their aunt, the duchesse d'Angoulême (the king's childless daughter-in-law). These survivors of the Revolution were obsessed with the future of the French monarchy and the heir to the throne. Little Henri was not just Maria Carolina's son, he belonged to the kingdom, and his deeds and actions became a constant excuse for propaganda.

Thus the young duc de Bordeaux was paraded at Bagatelle before the Swiss Guards, just as the king of Rome had been exhibited in the arms of his father, Napoleon. Formerly a symbol of indomitable adolescence, Bagatelle once again became a setting for innocent youth. This youth embodied hopes for perpetuity and the future of the monarchy. Both those hopes were shattered by the march of history, victim of the blind mistakes made by those who refused to see reality.

Paradoxically, the endless accounts of royal hunts published in the press, like the display of the children at Bagatelle, tended to tarnish the image of the restored monarchy by crediting the idea that the real center of power was no longer the king but parliament. As Sosthène de La Rochefoucauld, the historic aide-de-camp to the comte d'Artois, named director of the Beaux-Arts in 1824, realized with great lucidity, "The king is never seen anywhere, never goes to the theater, and although he works more than any other prince, *Le Moniteur* ... continues to report: 'The king went hunting, and the Royal Children of France were at Bagatelle.'"[142]

Bagatelle turned against its creator. Despite undeniable successes, notably in the spheres of art and diplomacy, Charles X's reign ended a few years later in a terrible setback. On July 25, 1830, after appointing a governing cabinet headed by Jules de Polignac—none other than the son of the duchesse de Polignac, Marie Antoinette's favorite—Charles X issued a set of decrees known as the Saint-Cloud Ordinances, which dissolved parliament, summoned the electoral college (all the while changing the electoral system), and suspended freedom of the press. The subsequent uprising—the "Three Glorious Days" of July 27, 28, and 29—forced the royal family to emigrate to England and brought the reign to an end. Believing he could abdicate in favor of his grandson, Charles X in fact left the field open to another pretender, his cousin the duc d'Orléans, who ascended to the throne as King Louis-Philippe.

With panache, the duchesse de Berry tried to spur an insurrection in the Vendée region in favor of her son, but the attempt failed miserably. Young Henri was driven away from his own country at the age of ten and would spend the rest of his life in exile. After the Second Empire fell in 1870, he had one last chance to accede to the throne, but he failed to grasp it.[143]

Charles X, meanwhile, most often found himself "on the wrong side of history." In his youth he compromised the finances as well as the image of the monarchy and the reputation of Marie Antoinette; when the Revolution first broke out, he joined ranks with those rejecting the moderate solution of a constitutional monarchy; during his reign, he was blind to social and political changes underway in France; and finally, during his exile, he and the duchesse d'Angoulême confined his grandson Henri to the intellectual and moral prison of absolute monarchy, clinging to the sole hope of an impossible return to the ancien régime.

Louis-Philippe, upon becoming "King of the French," did not take possession of Bagatelle. Known for his "stone addiction," his obsession with building projects, he had acquired the château de Neuilly in 1817 in exchange for the stables at the Palais-Royal in Paris, which he

FACING PAGE
The main door on Bagatelle's courtyard façade following restoration. As German architect Friedrich Gilly described so precisely in 1798, "The panels of the doors are fitted with grilles of matte bronze and, with the fanlight above, give light to the vestibule."

PAGES 178–79
Jean-Charles Joseph Rémond and Francisque Grenier de Saint-Martin, *The Young Comte de Bordeaux in Front of the Bagatelle Pavilion, Near Paris*, oil on canvas, 1826 (Musée Carnavalet – Histoire de Paris, Paris). The acts and deeds of the young duc de Bordeaux, heir to the throne under the name of Henri V, were staged right from infancy, notably during military parades at Bagatelle.

sold to the Crown. Louis-Philippe then considerably enlarged and improved his Neuilly estate, so his interest in nearby Bagatelle was probably limited. Furthermore, when a law was passed on February 17, 1832, establishing a new civil list, parliament reduced the size of the royal household and its budget, which dropped from eighteen to twelve million francs per year. Fontaine, the invincible national architect, was scandalized:

> "[T]he Rambouillet estate ... has been withdrawn from the royal endowment and given to the State. The château de Versailles, like those in Compiègne and Fontainebleau, remain stripped and shorn of all the outbuildings that, long detached or otherwise from the royal residence, are not part of its direct service. The château and grounds of Bagatelle, which should be seen as a small division of the Bois de Boulogne and as a hunting lodge, has been handed over to the ministry of finances to be sold or rented out.... The parliamentary majority ... thought it could save money and flatter the country by voting to make the monarch as poor as possible.[144]

An English traveler noted his impression of a visit to Bagatelle in a diary entry dated June 9, 1834:

> This evening we drove to Bagatelle, in the Bois de Boulogne. It is another of the royal residences before the Revolution, or, I may rather say, a retreat, as the house consists only of an entrance hall, an immense and beautiful saloon, with a dining room on one side and a billiard room on the other, hardly any bedrooms above, and these very small, low and confined. It must have been used chiefly as a banqueting-house. The grounds and park, consisting of forty acres, are laid out with great taste, and form a delightful spot. An artificial piece of water, supplied by an aqueduct from the neighboring Seine, flows through majestic rocks, under Chinese bridges, and round constructed islands, till it appears again in the shape of a cascade.... After the restoration, it was a favorite retreat of the duc de Berry, and now belongs to the duc de Bordeaux, though the new régime has appropriated it to the State. Two attempts have been made to sell it by auction; but as the land is bad, and the expenses of repairing and keeping up the place would be very great, no buyers appeared at the set price of 300,000 fr.[145]

The third attempt to sell the property succeeded: just a few months later, Bagatelle was bought by the 4th Marquess of Hertford. Although born in England, Lord Hertford had spent most of his life in France and was an enthusiastic collector of eighteenth-century French art. The comte d'Artois's pleasure house was about to become a temple of art and beauty.

FACING PAGE
A view of the music room leading to the dining room, whose original ceiling, painted by Bélanger, was replaced by an imitation sky in the nineteenth century. The panels of grotesques in stucco were ornamented by medallions painted by Dugourc to imitate alabaster bas-reliefs set against marble.

PAGES 182–83
Current view of the entrance to the main courtyard. Preceded by their own small, circular courtyard adorned with statues, the two guard houses were built in 1872–73 to replace the Pages' Pavilion, damaged during the Paris Commune. The house with compass rose (on the left) and the one with clock (right) flank two remarkable trees, a *Platanus × acerifolia* (London plane) and *Platanus orientalis* (Oriental plane).

IAPIAN
INDEPENDANTE
AFRIQUE
MER DES INDES
OCEAN
TERRES AUSTRALES

Chapter 6

Bagatelle Saved by Englishmen

The Treasures of Hertford and Wallace

"Lord Hertford is assuredly the greatest collector in Europe."

William Bürger, "Les Collections Particulières," *Paris Guide*, 1867

"The most striking characteristic of the collection, after its variety and magnificence, is its genial, easy, unexclusive taste—the good nature of well-bred opulence."

Henry James, *The Atlantic Monthly*, 1873

From 1835 to 1905 the story of Bagatelle was closely tied to the fate of the Seymour-Conway family, marquesses of Hertford. It is the sad tale of an aristocratic line that ended in dissoluteness and isolation after just a few generations, yet it is also the wonderful genesis of the creation of one of the most important and perhaps largest collections of art ever to be assembled in the nineteenth century.

This "English" chapter in Bagatelle's history can be traced back to the unexpected and intimate relationship that the Seymour-Conways built with France, which made the 4th Marquess and his heir, Richard Wallace, true Frenchmen by adoption. Lord Hertford bought Bagatelle on September 22, 1835, and spent much of his life there until he passed away on August 25, 1870. He died in the bedroom of the comte d'Artois overlooking the main courtyard and Seine, exactly one week after Napoleon III lost the battle of Sedan, bringing down the Second Empire. Hertford's ilegitimate son, private secretary, and principal legatee, Sir Richard Wallace, died twenty years later in the same bed in that same bedroom, owner of a vast fortune and a henceforth famous art collection, part of which would become the Wallace Collection in London in 1906. Two Englishmen in France, two lives spent between London, Paris, and Bagatelle: lives full of turmoil, adventure, tragedy, and beauty.

The prodigiously rich Seymour-Conway family was highly prominent at the court of George III and remained so during the Regency in the early nineteenth century.[146] The 1st Marquess of Hertford, Francis Seymour-Conway, nephew of Sir Robert Walpole, was ambassador to France, Lord Lieutenant of Ireland, and finally, Lord Chamberlain from 1766 to 1782.[147] The 2nd Marquess, Francis Ingram Seymour-Conway, was also a leading figure, not only because he was a politician who served as ambassador to Berlin as well as Lord Chamberlain from 1812 to 1821, but above all thanks to his second wife, Isabella, with whom the Prince Regent was infatuated. Up to the early 1820s the regent, the marquess, and the marchioness would dine as a "threesome" in the Hertford residence on Manchester Square in London, sparking wild rumors in the British press.

The 2nd Marquess and his wife were the family's first great collectors. They acquired eighteenth-century French furniture, "contemporary" British painting, Flemish masterpieces, and large *vedute*, or views, by Canaletto. The situation was particularly favorable, because the French Revolution and Empire, with all the reversals of fortune they triggered, brought entire collections to the market, creating many buying opportunities for Britain's wealthiest families.

However, unexpected events unfolded, such that the Seymour-Conways' destiny would permanently lean toward France. Francis Charles, the only son of the 2nd Marquess, was notorious in the 1790s for his extravagant lifestyle, numerous mistresses, debauched parties, and penchant for gambling: a Georgian version of the comte d'Artois!

Aged twenty-one, burdened with debts, Francis Charles met a young Italian woman, Maria Fagnani—known as Mie-Mie—who was the offspring of a furtive encounter between an Italian aristocrat and Lord March, Duke of Queensberry. Dubbed "Old Q," the duke was a rich London bachelor, and agreed to take charge of the child, entrusting her upbringing to his friend George Selwyn, another notorious bachelor and leading member of parliament. When Francis Charles secretly married Mie-Mie in 1798, the duke agreed to pay off the bridegroom's debts and make the newlyweds his legatees.

PAGE 185
This bronze reproduction of Charles-Auguste Lebourg's terracotta *Bust of Richard Wallace* (1869) was given to the Fondation Mansart by the Society of the Wallace Fountains, for the fountains that had been introduced to Paris in 1872.

FACING PAGE
Étienne Carjat, *Richard Seymour-Conway, 4th Marquess of Hertford*, photograph, c. 1860 (Wallace Collection, London). Lord Hertford bought Bagatelle in 1835. This rare portrait shows him wearing the insignia of the Order of the Garter, bestowed on him in 1846.

PAGES 188–89
Benjamin Zix, *Le Boulevard des Italiens*, pen and ink and wash, c. 1802 (private collection). Richard Seymour-Conway spent his childhood and adolescence in Paris. His mother, Mie-Mie, moved there in 1802, after the peace of Amiens, in a house that dominated the corner of boulevard des Italiens and rue Cerutti, nowadays rue Laffitte.

MAGASIN DE

Unfortunately, the couple's relationship soon went sour. After the birth of a daughter and a first son (named Richard), Francis Charles turned back to his mistresses and his gambling rooms. Mie-Mie, who was never accepted by either her parents-in-law or the British landed gentry, took advantage of a trip to Paris in 1802 to leave her husband and settle in France with their children.

At "Old Q's" place in Richmond she had befriended many French aristocrats in exile. Henceforth a titled lady with an independent fortune,[148] she easily fit into Empire society, and never left France again. Thus Richard Seymour-Conway, the future 4th Marquess and future owner of Bagatelle, spent his childhood and teenage years in Paris. At the insistence of his father, he was obliged to return to England for his education in 1816, but after a few years he went back to his mother and his half-brother, "Lord Henry," in their Paris apartment on boulevard des Italiens.[149]

In London, the 3rd Marquess managed to pull off skillful operations that increased the family fortune. He was universally recognized as a man of taste and for a while he was a faithful companion to the regent, advising him on the art market. He acquired for his future king the famous Rembrandt portrait of the Rijcksen couple (*The Shipbuilder and His Wife*), now one of the gems in the British Royal Collection.[150] Thanks to shrewd purchases, Francis Charles also enriched his family's own collection with major works by Dutch old masters and the likes of van Dyck, Titian, Gainsborough, and Reynolds.[151]

In the political sphere however, his career was a failure. Considered unscrupulous and unreliable, suspected of underhanded financial dealings, Francis Charles was swiftly forgotten by the Tory party. He retreated into a sybaritic lifestyle and was dubbed "the Caliph of Regent's Park" by the British press, after he built a vast residence in that new London neighborhood and gave legendary parties there.[152] The final years of his life were devoted to pleasure and dissolution, surrounded by greedy servants and mistresses who would be accused of embezzling part of his fortune. Francis Charles's setback in England certainly encouraged his son Richard to remain in France. Richard was comfortably set-up in Paris, where he was simply called "Lord Hertford."

In Paris, Mie-Mie experienced the tragic death of her daughter, but found solace in the company of a young lad of six on whom she turned her affection. Named Richard Jackson, the boy was apparently the product of an affair between her son, Lord Hertford, and one Agnes Jackson, which took place in England when Hertford was just eighteen. Mie-Mie decided to adopt the child. She referred to him as "my nephew," and he called her "Aunt Mie-Mie." The little Jackson boy grew up to be Richard Wallace, first becoming Hertford's private secretary, later his trusted agent on the art market, and finally, in 1870, his legatee.

Lord Hertford had no other children. In 1834 he met a certain Mademoiselle Bréart, from a family of Franco-British intellectuals, and took her to London for a "wedding." The ceremony was a sham, designed to fool the young lady. She nevertheless remained Hertford's companion under the name of Madame Oger, but never gave birth to an heir. So the son of "the Caliph of Regent's Park" had a mistress, but no family. This was the end of the line for one of the most powerful British families of the early nineteenth century. With no role at the British court and no legitimate heir, Lord Hertford could focus on his sole passion—collecting works of art.

Paris was then the leading center of intellectual life in Europe. "For real pleasure, there is nothing in my mind comparable to the Salons of Paris. It is the only place where statesmen, men

FACING PAGE
Jean-Baptiste Greuze, *A Young Woman Praying at the Altar of Love*, oil on canvas, 1767 (Wallace Collection, London). Originally owned by the duc de Choiseul, this painting figured in a scene on his famous snuffbox. Having later belonged to the comte d'Artois and then to Cardinal Fesch, the painting was bought by Lord Hertford in 1845.

of science and literature and men of good society can meet together regularly to exchange ideas and opinions. Paris is undoubtedly the intellectual capital of the world."[153] In October 1840, during a single stroll along the boulevards of Paris, composer Franz Liszt ran into the likes of Heinrich Heine, Honoré de Balzac, Frédéric Chopin, and Hector Berlioz. Cafés were the perfect place to socialize, notably Café Tortoni on the corner of rue Taitbout and boulevard des Italiens, just across the street from the Café de Paris. "If you have not seen the Café de Paris.... in 1840, you have seen nothing." That was where the famous writer Alfred de Musset ate veal stew three times a week—and Mie-Mie and her family happened to live just above it.[154]

Lord Hertford therefore found himself at the center of the universe. His annual income from his British and Irish properties made him one of the richest men of the day. Very well trained by his father, he was extremely cultured, and had shrewd judgment and loyal advisers. The art market was booming, and Hertford made purchase after purchase.

The reigns of Louis XVIII, Charles X, and Louis-Philippe were haunted by a veritable nostalgia for the past. The duchesse de Berry's penchant for the French Gothic revival— known as the *troubadour* style—had helped to make the Middle Ages fashionable. Starting in the 1830s, the leading ladies who set the tone, such as Madame de Flauhaut and the comtesse Le Hon,[155] began to fill their apartments with "period" furniture and objects. Even King Louis-Philippe would visit the antique shops. Everyone collected. Eighteenth-century items, however, were not yet fashionable. At court, the king's youngest daughter, Marie d'Orléans, embodied the sensibility of the day. She was an artist who was passionately interested in Joan of Arc, and the sculptures she produced of her heroine became icons of Louis-Philippe's reign. When writing letters, Marie would sit in her "medieval" armchair, which she "adored" and which drew admiration from artist Ary Scheffer.[156] In the same spirit, the Paris mansion built by James de Rothschild at 19 rue Laffitte favored medieval and Renaissance styles; the highlight was its François-I reception room, featuring Gothic-revival furnishings and fireplaces.[157]

Lord Hertford himself, however, remained faithful to family tradition and, to a certain extent, to the English taste that had reigned since the early Regency period. He built his collection by concentrating on French objets d'art of the previous century, preferably with a royal provenance; and when it came to paintings, he acquired many Flemish and Dutch masterpieces, like his father. Yet the 4th Marquess was not just an English collector living in Paris, he was also, and perhaps firstly, a French collector. As such, he was interested in contemporary artists while also being keen on eighteenth-century French painting, notably in its "voluptuous and elitist version," a taste very much aligned with his collection of decorative arts in the rococo fashion, notably Sèvres porcelain from the Louis-XV period.[158] Relentlessly acquiring works by Watteau, Boucher, and Greuze, he helped to pioneer the rediscovery of this "French school," whose key works were still being ignored or disparaged, and whose prices were well below what they would fetch in the 1860s to 1880s.[159]

It was not until 1859 that the Goncourt brothers started to publish *L'Art du XVIIIe Siècle* (Art of the Eighteenth Century), and only in 1860 was the first major exhibition of such art held.[160] Organized by the Martinet gallery, the show called on the greatest private art-lovers of the day, and unsurprisingly, Lord Hertford was among the key lenders. His two masterpieces by Boucher, *Sunrise* and *Sunset*, painted for Madame de Pompadour, were admired by all. The same

FACING PAGE
Louis Tocqué, *Portrait of Louis Philippe d'Orléans, duc de Chartres*, oil on canvas (private collection). Once thought to be a portrait of the comte d'Artois by Jean-Marc Nattier, it held pride of place in the interior of Bagatelle in the late nineteenth century. Like many other masterpieces there, it was acquired by art dealer Jacques Seligmann in 1914 and is now in a private collection in the United States.

PAGE 195
Jean-Honoré Fragonard, *The Swing*, oil on canvas, c. 1767–68 (Wallace Collection, London). Fragonard's masterpiece, now the pride of the Wallace Collection, was bought by Lord Hertford at the auction of the duc de Morny collection in 1865.

"He bows before the superiority of sixteenth-century masters, but he is fond above all of the Louis-XIV, Louis-XV, and Louis-XVI periods. France should be pleased at this, and should be particularly grateful to Hertford, because more than anyone else he has helped, for example, to bring back into favor eighteenth-century art, which had been totally discredited."

Gazette des Beaux-Arts, January 1, 1873

exhibition also featured Fragonard's *The Swing*, then owned by the duc de Morny but bought by Hertford five years later at the duke's estate sale. The painting was destined to become one of the most famous of the eighteenth century, and today still graces the Wallace Collection.[161]

In its January 1873 issue, the *Gazette des Beaux-Arts* stressed the innovative aspect of Hertford's taste:

> He bowed before the superiority of sixteenth-century masters, but he was fond above all of the Louis-XIV, Louis-XV, and Louis-XVI periods. France should be pleased at this, and should be particularly grateful to Hertford, because more than anyone else he has helped, for example, to bring back into favor eighteenth-century art, which had been totally discredited; its rare admirers were even mocked, and disdain extended to the most illustrious members of that school, including Watteau himself! ... I cannot forget the reception Lord Hertford received after the Laffitte sale, where he had just paid 12,000 francs for a head by Greuze. 12,000 francs for a Greuze! Only an Englishman could be so mad. The jeers rained down. The truth is that the marquess had very sure taste, and was always ahead of the opinion of other art lovers, so that the one who was ridiculed at the start soon managed to lay down the law through his excellent purchases, most of which are notable for that stamp of elegance—that delightful, pleasant nature, that refined grace, that exquisite charm and whiff of flirtatiousness—which all eighteenth-century masters, major and minor, were able to instill in their works, of whatever nature.[162]

How should we interpret the difficulty Louis-Philippe's administration had in selling Bagatelle, which remained on the market for nearly three years. Was it too closely associated with memories of the Bourbon monarchs who had emigrated? Was it too small to be considered a real house? Perhaps it was that very diminutiveness, that modesty, which finally convinced Hertford to take the plunge. The estate suited not only his appetite for the eighteenth century, but also the use he intended to make of it—a private haven rather than a place for parties.

In this respect, a comparison with James de Rothschild is revealing. As a representative of the banking dynasty in France, Rothschild decided to buy the château de Boulogne in 1817 and the château de Ferrières in 1829. In addition to the work on his Paris mansion at 19 rue Laffitte, in the late 1850s he had both châteaux rebuilt at great expense. For their interior decoration he hired Eugène Lami, who favored the Louis-XIV revival style. At Ferrières in particular, the lavishness of the decoration matched the scale of the palace—the main hall could practically contain all of Bagatelle! The grandeur of architectural projects indeed reflects social ambitions, and James de Rothschild's ambitions were unrivaled. In contrast, when it came to accumulating masterpieces, Hertford seemed the more ambitious of the two. Emblematic in this regard was his purchase of the *The Laughing Cavalier* by Frans Hals, another masterpiece now in the Wallace Collection. This portrait, surely one of the finest Flemish paintings of the seventeenth century, triggered an epic bidding war between the two collectors when it was auctioned at the Pourtalès-Gorgier sale in 1865. The hammer price of 51,000 francs, paid by Hertford, was considered exorbitant at the time. Rothschild was an authentic art lover, of course, but he sought above all to consolidate his family standing and social rank.[163] With Hertford, art counted most. When it came to everything else, Bagatelle sufficed. *Parva sed apta!*

FACING PAGE
Étienne Meslier, *View of Bagatelle*, pencil and stump, c. 1835 (Musée Carnavalet – Histoire de Paris, Paris). The view of the Pages' Pavilion, taken from the route de Sèvres, suggests the state of neglect of Bagatelle when it was bought by Lord Hertford.

PAGES 198–99
During the Second Empire (1852–70), Charles Marville produced an album of photos titled *Bagatelle up to 1870* (Musée Carnavalet – Histoire de Paris, Paris). This set of forty-five albumin prints from wet-collodion glass negatives reveals the condition of the pavilion just prior to the major renovation that would alter Bélanger's original façade. Here, the courtyard façade still featured a large glass porch sheltering the entrance steps.

PARVA SED APTA

ABOVE
The Three Graces, detail of a panel on a door to the Hubert Robert bathroom. The panel faithfully reflects the spirit of late eighteenth-century "grotesque" decoration, but the style of the faces indicates repainting done during the Restoration (1815–30) or July Monarchy (1830–48).

FACING PAGE
The main drawing room during the Second Empire, photographed by Charles Marville (albumin print from wet-collodion glass negative, c. 1860–70, Musée Carnavalet – Histoire de Paris, Paris). With its plush, central sofa and accumulation of objets d'art, clocks, and mantelpiece decorations, the heavily furnished music room (then called the "dome room"), reflected the lavish decoration of Second-Empire style, of which Lord Hertford was an early fan.

PAGES 202–3
Detail of a painted panel on the door of the bathroom.

LEFT
Bagatelle seen from the garden, photographed by Charles Marville (albumin print from wet-collodion glass negative, c. 1860, Musée Carnavalet – Histoire de Paris, Paris). The French window to the right of the curved drawing room indicates that the comte d'Artois's notorious secret boudoir had not yet been eliminated.

The comte d'Artois's little pleasure house, so loved by the duc de Berry, whose children grew up there, had been neglected ever since the Bourbons emigrated and was, unfortunately, in poor condition. Thomas Raikes, a banker, dandy, and famous diarist, was passing through Paris when his friend Hertford invited him to have a look at the new purchase. Raikes described the visit in his journal on March 1, 1836:

> I went this morning with Yarmouth [i.e., Hertford] to look at his new purchase of Bagatelle, where he is repairing and improving the whole domain. He is building a range of greenhouses on the model of those at Chiswick and adding to the plantations. There is a large steam-engine which supplies the house, the offices, the ponds and the cascade with water from the Seine.... The dry rot has unfortunately made its way into the house, and it has become necessary to lay down new floorings in all the rooms, ... which is the more to be regretted as it must injure the beautiful painted ceilings of the principal apartments. We detected some remains of the fresco paintings in the boudoir, which were done by the order of the comte d'Artois, and form a great contrast to the present devout habits of Charles X. When completely restored..., it will be the most beautiful fairy retreat in France, at only a quarter of an hour's drive from the capital.[164]

Apart from this rare account, we remain unaware of the exact extent of work done after Hertford bought Bagatelle. Whatever the case, that work represented the start of a long series of changes that would significantly affect the appearance of the premises:

- Sometime during the 1860s—probably 1864—Hertford asked architect Léon de Sanges to raise the height of the château, thereby making the upper floor more comfortable; this resulted in a significant alteration of the courtyard façade.
- During the same period, de Sanges also erected new, larger stables on the other side of the main entrance to the grounds. These buildings, which can still be seen today, were done in the vernacular, red-brick style, apparently to match the "chalet style" used by Davioud for the entrance to the Bois de Boulogne.[165] The water pump, which also survives, was also rebuilt in a "mixed" revival style of Louis-XIII inspiration.
- In 1871, Richard Wallace, having just inherited the property from Lord Hertford, built the rococo Louis-XV style pavilion that still stands at the entrance to the grounds.
- Finally, in 1872–73, Wallace demolished the Pages' Pavilion, which had been damaged during the events of the Paris Commune, and replaced it by two small guards' pavilions flanking the lane leading toward the château. To the right of this lane, a new building, dubbed Trianon, was built in a Gabriel-revival style to harmonize with the château's new façade. The domestic staff formerly housed in the Pages' Pavilion were moved to quarters underneath the main terrace opposite the Trianon, overlooking what is today "la route de Sèvres à Neuilly."

Paradoxically, it was the English owners of Bagatelle who stripped the comte d'Artois's country retreat of its typically British Palladian appearance, replacing it with a French neoclassical one. It is perfectly understandable that Lord Hertford should want a more comfortable, modern home where he could really live. And the new style he adopted corresponded, in general, to

PAGES 206–7
View of the dome's "fish-scale" tiles of zinc.

FACING PAGE
This rococo Louis-XV pavilion was built at the ceremonial entrance to the grounds of Bagatelle in 1871 on the instructions of Richard Wallace, who had just inherited the estate from Lord Hertford.

PAGE 210
G. Maurage, *Detail of a Dormer Window on the Stables at Bagatelle*, published in *Moniteur des Architectes*, 1874, plate 33. Architect Léon de Sanges built new stables by the Sèvres road entrance. Vernacular in style, these red-brick buildings accorded with the "chalet style" used by Davioud for the entrance to the Bois de Boulogne.

PAGE 211
The stables today, glimpsed through the trees.

MONITEUR DES ARCHITECTES

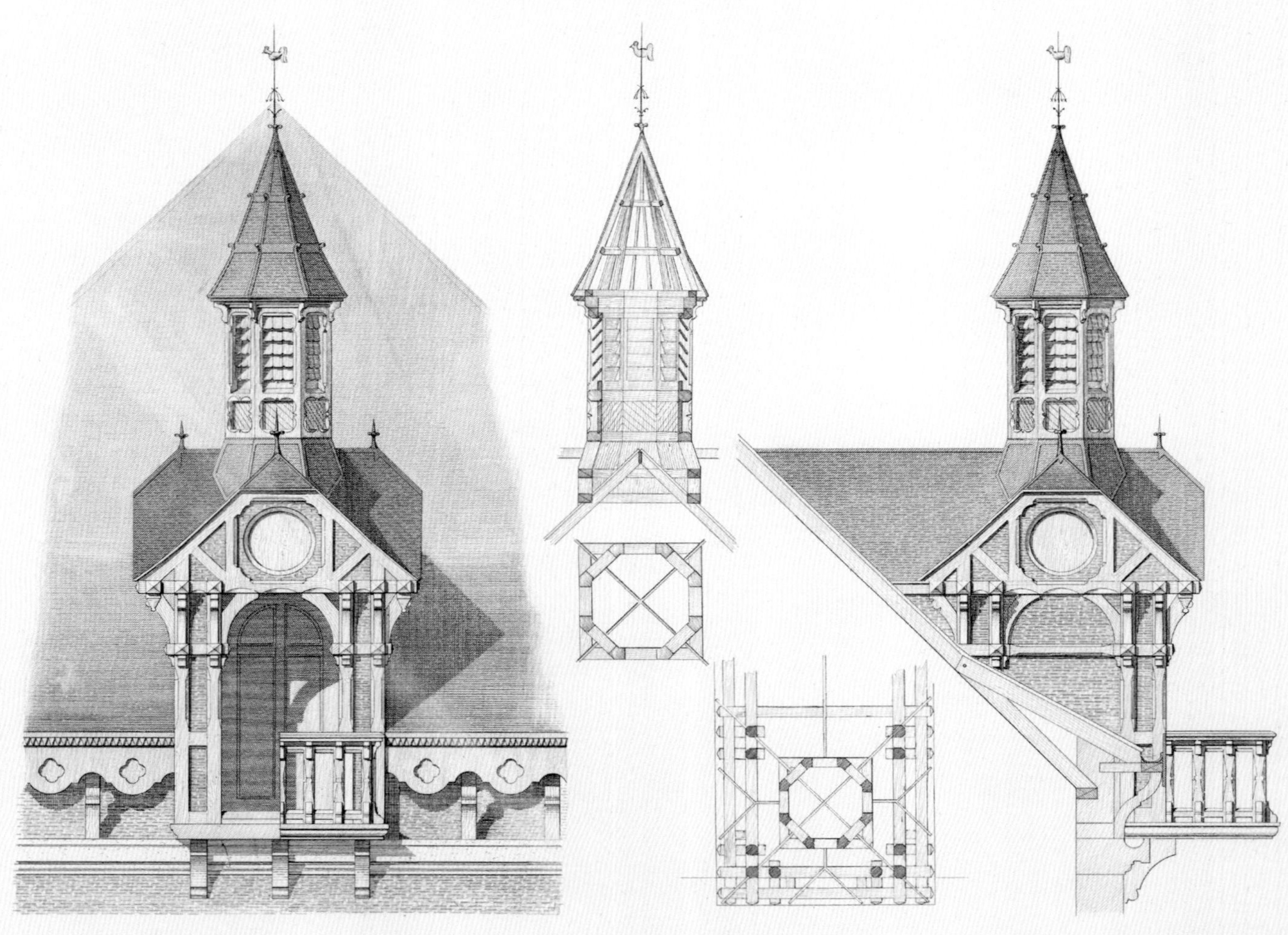

ECURIES DU CHATEAU DE BAGATELLE

DÉTAIL DE LUCARNE

M. L. DE SANGES, ARCHITECTE

Echelle de o^m,oc

CHÂTEAU DE BAGATELLE

Façade

pr mètre

(BOIS DE BOULOGNE)

rincipale.

his enthusiasm for eighteenth-century France—Gabriel's Petit Trianon at Versailles seems to have been the main source of inspiration throughout. The new owners would nevertheless be criticized for sacrificing the uniqueness of Bélanger's work, and for altering the symmetry of the premises by replacing the centrally aligned Pages' Pavilion with the off-center Trianon.[166]

And what of the interior? With his precocious, pronounced taste for French painting and decorative arts of the eighteenth century, Hertford pioneered the "Louis-XVI revival" that emerged during the Second Empire (1852–70), as illustrated by photographs of Bagatelle taken by Charles Marville in the 1860s. One visitor described the ground-floor entrance hall as follows: the walls are clad with white marble; green veined-marble vases, with gilt bronze ram's heads as handles, stand on the two low gray marble columns at the side of the entrance door. On the stove, also decorated with ram's heads (still extant), was an impressive display piece, in which three one-third life-size figures are placed back-to-back, a mercury and two female effigies, one with cudgel, sword, and scale, and the other with torch and laurel branch. The appearance of these decorative pieces against the background of the white marble wall creates an impressive effect.[167]

To the right, the billiard room was renamed the "music room" in honor of a musical clock there. This room contained a Boulle-style desk and a large round table whose leg was also adorned with Boulle marquetry and gilt-bronze mounts in the shape of dolphins—hence was assumed to have probably belonged to the dauphin. In fact, it was of recent English manufacture. There was also an early eighteenth-century chest of drawers, while a clock and a barometer hung on the wall were said to surpass everything of the kind in the Hertford collection in delicacy of workmanship and elegance of structure.

What was called the "dome room" (the main drawing room now known as the music room), held two large cabinets from the Boulle workshop, decorated with medallions bearing the inscription *Ludovicus Magnus Rex*, and a large desk in the style of Reisener. There were also the candelabras and clock seen in a photo taken by Marville in 1857. Finally, the masterwork in the room was Houdon's sculpted portrait of Sophie Arnould, now in the Louvre.

The Callet boudoir was called "the comte d'Artois boudoir" after a painting that evoked the château's founder. This alleged portrait of Artois by Nattier—of which Hertford was apparently very fond—is now attributed to Louis Tocqué and in fact shows the duc de Chartres, a childhood friend of the count, who would become Philippe-Égalité during the Revolution.

Finally, there was the red boudoir, that is to say the bathroom that formerly housed paintings by Hubert Robert; its ceiling was considerably higher since the secret, mezzanine-level lair described in Bachaumont's memoirs had been eliminated. The red boudoir held a child's desk, a Louis-XVI style sofa, and two Régence-style cabinets. Two paintings were mentioned: one, by Boucher, showed bathing nymphs, while the other, also by Boucher, was oval in shape and took up most of the ceiling, featuring nymphs occupied with flowers, accompanied by putti, nowadays in the collections of the Gulbenkian Foundation.[168]

The visitor mentioned just a few artworks, the ones he felt best characterized Bagatelle, whereas there were over one hundred paintings, drawings, and prints, some twenty-five Sèvres vases, and numerous masterpieces of sculpture, notably by Houdon—the photo of the terrace taken by Marville records the presence of Houdon's famous allegorical figure, *Winter*, now in the Metropolitan Museum in New York. Bagatelle was thus a veritable museum, a compendium

PAGES 212–13
Sergent, *Château de Bagatelle, Bois de Boulogne—Main Façade [of the Trianon]*, engraving published in *Moniteur des Architectes*, 1876, plate 49. Built in a Gabriel-revival style to harmonize with the château's new façade, the Trianon was designed by architect Léon de Sanges at Richard Wallace's request.

FACING PAGE
Housselin, *Water Pump at the Château de Bagatelle*, engraving published in *Moniteur des Architectes*, 1873, plate 29. Rebuilt in a Louis-XIII revival spirit, the water pump still exists. It pumped water from the Seine up to the high rock in the park.

of French artistic treasures from the eighteenth and nineteenth centuries. But those treasures were jealously guarded by Lord Hertford. Although he willingly lent some items to temporary exhibitions, such as the one on Marie Antoinette held in the Petit Trianon in 1867,[169] he rarely welcomed visitors to the premises. According to the Goncourt brothers, the new owner of Bagatelle was a miserly misanthrope, a recluse who received no guests. "There have never been more miserly millions than those of the noble lord.... A complete, absolute, unashamed monster, even more of a monster than his brother Seymour, who redeemed the black wickedness of his family with certain generous qualities. It is Lord Hertford who is given to making the dreadful remark: 'Men are evil, and when I die I shall at least have the consolation of knowing that I have never rendered anyone a service.'"[170]

Is that a fair portrait? Probably in part, when Hertford was sapped by illness toward the end of the 1860s.[171] But the picture should be nuanced when it comes to the 1840s and 1850s. The marquess was particularly active on the art market and his presence was noted everywhere. Journalist Henri Rochefort described him as follows:

> The Marquess of Hertford was the opposite of lavish. He wore a frock coat that was almost shiny, and buttoned up to the neck, as though to hide the secret lack of a shirt. I never glimpsed the least scrap of linen peeking out from a black cravat worn very high, resembling the horsehair collars worn by retired officers on half-pay. Nor was his hat brilliant; or rather, it was *too* brilliant, to the point of casting coppery reflections on his obscure defamers. For that matter, he used the hat like a telegraph between himself and the auctioneers who, when he raised his hand to it, knew that this silent gesture equaled a bid.[172]

Hertford had been close to Louis-Napoleon Bonaparte before the latter became emperor, and he seemed fully integrated into court life. When Horace de Viel Castel described the imperial couple's usual guests at festive hunting sojourns at the château de Compiègne, Hertford was among them. In her private memoirs, Madame Carette described a party at which they played La Corde Sensible ("Heartstrings"): "Through little epigrams, the quirks and foibles dear to those present would be revealed.... Monsieur de Morny began, referring to himself. Then it was a question of Lord Hertford. On hearing his name called out, the noble lord appeared somewhat flustered. Monsieur Mérimée, alluding to Hertford's charming residence in the Bois de Boulogne, asked Monsieur de Morny if it were true that the sole concern of this great and wealthy English lord was a 'Bagatelle.'"[173]

For that matter, Hertford was the only one to escape harsh criticism from Viel Castel, a curator at the Louvre known for his Anglophobia.

> The prince de Beauvau, who was of the party, is one of the most boring people I know. The prince de Bauffremont is a nonentity stitched up in the clothes of an old fop. The comte de Caumont La Force is a former pleasure-seeker of the wrong sort, whose wife was killed less than a year ago. The marquis de Caulaincourt is a good chap who lost an eye in the army, but of no account at all. Comte Frédéric de Lagrange combines a terrible reputation with total self-satisfaction. Baron Hallez-Claparède is as tiresome as autumn rain. Baron de Rothschild will perhaps entertain the assembly with his financial calculations, while Aubert and Meyerbeer will discuss music with Verdi, and Horace Vernet and Isabey will spout puns. The Marquess of Hertford is very witty.[174]

FACING PAGE
Despite the transformations of the nineteenth century, the Bagatelle pavilion still has the original sculpted overdoors made for the comte d'Artois.

PAGE 219
The music room, photographed by Charles Marville (albumin print from wet-collodion glass negative, c. 1860–70, Musée Carnavalet – Histoire de Paris, Paris). Henri-Léonard Wassmus made the Boulle-style armoire, another version of which was exhibited at the Universal Exposition of 1855 and bought by the Mobilier de la Couronne in June 1862; it still belongs to the Mobilier National and is currently at the château de Maisons.

"Through little epigrams, the quirks and foibles dear to those present would be revealed.... Monsieur de Morny began, referring to himself. Then it was a question of Lord Hertford. On hearing his name called out, the noble lord appeared somewhat flustered. Monsieur Mérimée, alluding to Hertford's charming residence in the Bois de Boulogne, asked Monsieur de Morny if it were true that the sole concern of this great and wealthy English lord was a 'Bagatelle.'"

Madame Carette, *Souvenir Intimes de la Cour des Tuileries, 1889–91*

PAGES 220–21
Charles Marville, *Lord Hertford, Madame Oger, and Richard Wallace on the Terrace of Bagatelle Pavilion*, photograph, c. 1858 (Musée Carnavalet – Histoire de Paris, Paris). Madame Oger, née Bréart, was duped into a phony marriage by Lord Hertford. She discovered the deceit, but nevertheless remained faithful to him for the rest of his life.

LEFT
The terrace of the Bagatelle pavilion, photographed by Charles Marville (albumin print from wet-collodion glass negative, c. 1860, Musée Carnavalet – Histoire de Paris, Paris). Visible on the terrace is an allegorical figure of Winter, Jean-Antoine Houdon's sculptural masterpiece, which belonged to the duc d'Orléans before being confiscated during the French Revolution. Lord Hertford acquired it in the 1840s; art dealer Jacques Seligmann later sold it to collector Henry Davison, whose wife donated it to the Metropolitan Museum of Art in New York in 1962.

Hertford's acquaintance with the emperor was moreover confirmed by another anecdote, again recounted by Viel Castel. Whether accurate or not, this highly surprising story demonstrates how close Hertford was to the court, as well as his reputation there:[175]

> Prince [Jérôme] Napoleon told his sister that Lord Hertford had given Comtesse Castiglione a million in order to sleep with her. He claimed to have heard it from Hertford himself, who got a receipt from the countess. Since a night that costs a million is an exceptional one, Hertford wanted to test the countess in all kinds of sensual pleasures. He was paying, and paying a great deal, hence intended to set his own rules. The countess had to undergo all the trials of the most refined libertinage—nothing was omitted. She spent three days in bed after that night, but today she seems to be completely recovered, and is more dazzling than ever.[176]

In another "exchange" reported by some biographers, Napoleon III apparently sought to buy Bagatelle from Hertford. To soften the blow of his refusal, the marquess allegedly promised the imperial family special access to the estate. That might explain the decision to install a riding ring—where the rose garden is today—for young prince Louis-Napoleon's riding lessons. Just above, Hertford erected a small building nearby, today called Le Bosquet de l'Impératrice (Empress Grove), which allowed Eugénie to monitor her son's progress.

Bagatelle thus received regular visits from the imperial family, several members of court, and a few friends and collectors sufficiently close to the marquess. Such visits were short, infrequent, and accorded to few, as recounted by Lady Eastlake in her diary. She and her husband, Sir Charles Lock Eastlake, director of the National Gallery and president of the Royal Academy, were among the leading lights of the British and European art world and were received everywhere. On a trip to Paris in 1860, they were entitled to see the Hertford treasures stashed on rue Laffitte, but no invitation came from Bagatelle. It was Wallace who organized the visit.

> Lord Hertford's son has kindly shown us his father's treasures here. He began by the garde-meuble, which is a story set apart to contain the spare furniture Lord Hertford has accumulated. A sort of stage has been erected in the center to accommodate the clocks alone, all of which are of the greatest beauty. The furniture is priceless; such things as would adorn, and have adorned, royal chambers in the most luxurious times. Then he took us into an entresol of the tiniest dimensions, looking out on the noisiest part of the Boulevards. There Lord Hertford lived for thirty-six years, thinking it a bore to move into his present gorgeous apartments. He made us sit down, with an easel before us, and handed us up a succession of small pictures of great value, which were piled on the floor.... Thence we went into Lord Hertford's apartments, which are laden with everything that inordinate wealth can buy, besides the finest pictures of the Dutch and Flemish schools. His Lordship is at Bagatelle, a country house in the Bois de Boulogne, which is also a depot of treasures.[177]

Therein lies the contradiction of the Hertford collection: a desire to own the finest works of art, but the same masterpieces piled on the floor, dozens of furnishings left in store, and magnificent but rarely visited galleries. A contradiction epitomized by Lady Eastlake's incomprehension and unease at not being invited to Bagatelle. It would take the personality of Wallace—the little

FACING PAGE
The "Pagodon," a pagoda-like gazebo placed on the grounds of Bagatelle by Lord Hertford, originally came from the Universal Exposition held in Paris in 1867. Bought in 1905, it was reinstalled in the Water Garden at Lord William Waldorf Astor's estate, Clivedon, in Buckinghamshire. A replica of this Chinese pagoda was erected in Bagatelle in 1996.

PAGES 226–27
A replica of the "Pagodon" was installed at Bagatelle in 1996.

Richard Jackson adopted at age six—to unveil to the world the treasures accumulated by three generations of Seymour-Conways. Viel Castel described that personality in 1851: "The Marquess of Hertford and Richard Wallace came to the Louvre; we visited all the modern sculpture rooms; the marquess wanted to have a mold and bronze cast made of a small marble group showing Prometheus. I took great pleasure in seeing Richard again, for I am truly fond of him. He is an excellent boy, an intelligent art lover, and together we have conducted many campaigns at auctions of curios."[178]

Wallace seemed much more open, more involved in the art world and society in the broader sense. During the Second Empire he collected art on his own account, but he acted above all as faithful agent and adviser to Hertford. Attending all public auctions, he became a veritable, widely recognized connoisseur of old masters. Yet he was also part of avant-garde circles. He frequented the salons hosted by Madame Sabatier, his lover for many years. These gatherings at the home of "La Présidente," as Sabatier was known, were attended by the cream of the Paris art world—Gustave Flaubert, Alfred de Musset, Théophile Gautier, the painter Ernest Meissonier, sculptors James Pradier and Auguste Clésinger, and many others. Wallace came to know the artists of the new French school. And he always remained loyal to the woman he loved. "Flaubert told me of La Présidente's unexpected fortune: she received title to 50,000 francs of annual income, two days before investment, sent by Richard Wallace, with whom she had slept in the past, and who had said to her, 'You'll see, if I ever become rich, I'll think of you.'"[179]

With his huge inheritance of 1870, Wallace's situation had indeed changed radically. He could take on a full place in society. Already, just a few weeks after Hertford died, as Paris came under siege by the Prussians, Wallace displayed his sense of duty by organizing a particularly efficient ambulance service, and he supplied financial and material support to destitute Parisians. He subsequently financed the installation of public drinking fountains in Paris that still bear his name—Wallace fountains—as well as the construction of the Hertford British Hospital, also in the French capital. He became the most generous, most popular philanthropist of his day. Every Parisian knew his name.[180]

Once peace returned to France, Wallace decided to go to England to assume responsibilities that neither the 3rd nor the 4th Marquess of Hertford had fulfilled. He went into politics, oversaw management of his Irish estates, frequently organized hunts for aristocratic society, and, of course, played his role of art patron to the full. Following the bombardment and occupation of Paris, not to mention the events of the Paris Commune, Wallace had decided to send part of his "French" collection to London, including certain items from Bagatelle. However, until his London residence, Hertford House, could be enlarged, there was no space for all those works. The opening of a new branch of the South Kensington Museum (now the Victoria and Albert Museum) in the working-class neighborhood of Bethnal Green in East London thus offered an unanticipated solution. The museum's directors, instead of displaying several private collections as originally intended, agreed to devote the premises entirely to the "Hertford collection." When it opened in 1872, the first exhibition catalog numbered 1,479 works, including 68 paintings and watercolors, 248 pieces of Sèvres porcelain, ten pieces of furniture and bronzes, 132 pieces of maiolica, and 111 miniatures. The last catalogue, published in 1875, included 2,400 works. The success of the undertaking matched its exceptional nature: 25,000 people entered the

FACING PAGE
John Thomson, *Sir Richard Wallace Holding one of his Pair of Bronze Statuettes of Flagellators (after Algardi and Duquesnoy)*, photograph, c. 1888 (National Portrait Gallery, London). Wallace was a learned connoisseur and one of the greatest collectors of his day. Here he holds a small bronze statuette that was exhibited in Bethnal Green in London in 1872.

museum on the first three days. During its three-year run, over 2.3 million visitors viewed the masterpieces collected by Hertford and Wallace.[181] It was an extraordinary, perhaps unique, event in the history of art. Henry James stressed, not without humor, the innovative aspect of the project. "Half in charity and (virtually) half in irony, a beautiful art collection has been planted in the middle of darkness and squalor—an experimental lever for the elevation of the masses."[182]

Despite this commitment to Bethnal Green, Wallace did not forget the French art scene. The new owner of Bagatelle, although henceforth living primarily in England, was thoroughly involved in the cultural life of Paris. Since 1864 he had been a member of the Union Centrale des Beaux-Arts Appliqués à l'Industrie, and in 1877 he joined the Association du Musée des Arts Décoratifs; when the Union Centrale des Arts Décoratifs was founded in 1878, he was among the most generous benefactors. Wallace often lent works to exhibitions, demonstrating the wealth and variety of his collection, which had been considerably enlarged by numerous purchases made in the 1870s. In 1874, Houdon's bust of Sophie Arnould—the masterpiece gracing Bagatelle's music room—was lent along with a set of paintings for a show designed to aid refugees from Alsace-Lorraine. In 1884, no fewer than twenty-five items from Bagatelle were lent to an historic exhibition, including a marble statue of Voltaire by Houdon, a terracotta group by Clodion, hardstone vases, Chinese cloisonné-enamel figurines, and an Egyptian statue in basalt.

The treasures of Bagatelle were thus displayed and shared with the public. But what of the château itself? The extent of work carried out testifies to Wallace's desire not only to maintain it but to use it. Did it therefore become a place of social gatherings and parties? A painting by Ferdinand Heilbuth, *A Party at Bagatelle*, which was exhibited in the Salon of 1883, depicts elegant, magnificently dressed women strolling in front of the Trianon; but the setting is partly imaginary, for there was never a lake nor dock below the terrace. The "party" itself appears fanciful. Although Heilbuth knew Wallace,[183] he seems to have worked from the lawn, as though he didn't have access to the Trianon itself. His painting is a vision of a party that one would have liked to have seen at Bagatelle but that probably never took place.

Like his father, Wallace spent his final days in the bedroom built for the comte d'Artois and died here. During his funeral, on July 23, 1890, the reporter from *L'Univers Illustré* first described the bier soberly installed on the ground floor of Bagatelle; then he followed the cortege, hailed by numerous onlookers who "respectfully took off their hats as the body passed by." The oration, delivered by a city councilor, Baudin, was reported thus:

> After having paid tribute to the philanthropist who made such noble use of his wealth throughout his life and notably during the terrible ordeals suffered by Paris twenty years ago, the speaker ended with these words: "Sir Richard Wallace lived discreetly, loved and admired by all these laboring people who have left their workshops today to pay him their respects. It is in the name of these people, and of this entire city, so deeply moved by the recollection of so many generous deeds, that I pay tribute to the memory of this good man, and express all my heartfelt sympathy to his family.[184]

FACING PAGE
The terrace and courtyard façade of the comte d'Artois's "pleasure house" following its restoration in 2012–22.

PAGES 232–33
Ferdinand Heilbuth, *A Party at Bagatelle*, oil on canvas, 1883 (galerie Ary Jan, Paris). Exhibited at the Salon of 1883, this painting shows elegant ladies in front of the Trianon. But the view is invented—there was never a lake nor dock below the terrace, and the artist's image is a poetic idealization.

Chapter 7

A Château and Some Roses

Celebrations and Cultural Heritage in the Twentieth Century

"I know not whether I shall be in a condition on Saturday to get up for a few hours and go to Bagatelle. I have cancelled all my outings this year, one after another, and I was saving this one in order to experience, in a single blossom, all those fragrances I failed to harvest. I hope and scarcely believe it—yet I would truly like to get there. And above all I would be so happy to get a glimpse of you, which I have not done for so many years."

Letter from Marcel Proust to the comtesse Greffulhe, 1909

On learning that Richard Wallace had died, Dowager Empress Victoria of Prussia wrote to her mother, Queen Victoria. "I saw in the papers yesterday by accident that Sir Richard Wallace is dead! How very sorry I am—he was a most generous and charitable man, & what a connoisseur and lover of art! I wonder what will become of all his fortune & who will have his splendid house and matchless collections in London, which I know so well and admire so much."[185]

The *Times* of London also reflected the widespread suspense generated by Wallace's death. "The ungracious question forces itself forward. What will happen to them [the works of art] now? He has left no child; his only son died three years ago, and common gossip has for a long time declared that he intended to leave everything to the nation, or to two nations. Hertford House and its content to England, the rest to France."[186]

What, then, would become of the Hertford-Wallace collection? In England, the answer to this question was simple; in France, it became a long saga. Take, for example, the fate of the portrait of the comte d'Artois so dear to Hertford: it changed hands eight times before the end of the twentieth century. Lady Wallace, who survived Richard by several years, made radically different decisions in her will concerning the two collections. Probably respecting her husband's wishes, she bequeathed the entire English collection to the British nation. This became the formidable Wallace Collection in London, where you can still admire a unique set of eighteenth-century French furniture, objets d'art, and paintings, as well as major masterworks of Dutch and Italian painting, significant Renaissance sculptures, one of the world's largest collections of armor, and many other treasures.

Most of the French collection and property, including Bagatelle, was bequeathed to Wallace's former private secretary, John Murray Scott, who remained very close to Lady Wallace after Sir Richard died. Scott in turn bequeathed most of his collection to Victoria Sackville-West. Sackville-West, nicknamed Petita or Lolo, was one of seven illegitimate children of Baron Lionel Sackville-West, her mother having been a Spanish dancer. (Pepita would marry her cousin, Lionel Edward Sackville-West, heir to the title of baron and to Knole House, a magnificent sixteenth- and seventeenth-century stately home in Kent, now open to the public.) After Lady Wallace died, Scott fell under Pepita's spell, remaining her devoted and unconditional admirer to the end of his days. Their apparently platonic relationship strangely echoes certain chapters in the Hertford saga a century earlier.

All this led to the total dispersion of Wallace's French possessions in the early twentieth century. In 1905, Scott decided to sell Bagatelle, which was bought, along with its grounds, by the City of Paris. As to the collection of artworks inherited by Lady Sackville in 1912, it was sold to the dealer Jacques Seligmann in a transaction that was one of the most spectacular deals ever done on the art market. Indeed, the bequest to Pepita was challenged by Scott's family. A lawsuit ensued, so the entire collection was sequestered in the old Wallace apartment at 2 rue Laffitte. Seligmann's son, Germain, described the extraordinary nature of the transaction in his biography. "The house on the rue Laffitte was under legal seal, and the objects it contain[ed] could not even be seen. Nevertheless, Jacques Seligmann entered into a legal covenant with Lady Sackville whereby, should she win the suit, he would become the sole and absolute owner of the entire French collection of Sir Richard Wallace at an agreed price.... At this point one must marvel at the instinct and courage of Jacques Seligmann, *for he had never seen the collection.*"[187]

PAGE 235
Detail of a painted panel on the door of the left-hand boudoir.

FACING PAGE
Sir Richard Wallace, photographed by Vernon Kaye, c. 1880. The philanthropic collector is sitting in the Large Gallery (now Great Gallery) of Hertford House, the London home he opened to visitors every year from May to July, starting in 1873. His widow, Lady Wallace, bequeathed it to the British nation in 1897, thereby establishing The Wallace Collection. Wallace's collection in France, however, suffered an entirely different fate, being dispersed at auction throughout the world.

PAGES 238–39
Current view of the upper floor of Bagatelle. The château is today empty—as it was just after the Revolution and again in the early twentieth century—awaiting the restoration and refurnishing of its interior.

ABOVE
The head gardener's house, with its typical red-brick façade and zinc roof, was built when Bagatelle's rose garden was laid out.

FACING PAGE
Henri Adolphe Laissement, *A Small Spot in the Rose Garden at Bagatelle*, oil on canvas, 1912 (private collection). Exhibited at the 1912 Salon de Paris, this painting evokes the early years of the rose garden at Bagatelle. After the City of Paris acquired the estate in 1905, the park service suggested the establishment of a collection of hardy and climbing plants that would appeal to ordinary visitors as well as garden enthusiasts.

The deal made the front page of the *New York Times*, which cited a price of 1.4 million dollars. In fact, Seligmann probably paid close to two million, solely on the basis of a handwritten list, without having inspected the works. But it was worth the risk. Sackville won her suit, the doors to the rue Laffitte apartment opened, and it is easy to imagine the dealer's sense of wonder and satisfaction as he discovered that he had pulled off the biggest deal of his career—perhaps one of the most lucrative transactions of the twentieth century. Germain described his father's first sight of the Wallace treasures formerly kept at Bagatelle:

> All over the floors, piled up in corners..., were some of the greatest sculptures of the eighteenth century and luxurious pieces of furniture made for the royal family. There, rolled in a corner, was the famous set of tapestries after cartoons by Boucher, now in the Philadelphia Museum. Standing on a table was a small marble figure by Lemoyne. Over there ... was the first version of Cupid bending his bow by Bouchardon. Yonder was the superb Houdon bust of Sophie Arnould, now in the Louvre at the bequest of Edouard Stern.[188]

There were also countless masterpieces of decorative art, "objects which exhibit such perfection of proportion, respect for the essence of the wood and the chiseling of gilded bronze; ... a table such as the Riesener, now in the Frick Collection, or a delicately conceived bit of bronze such as the Veil-Picard chandelier, now in the Louvre ... reveal a civilization which attained for a few years a pinnacle of refinement."[189] And the list went on: masterpieces by Houdon, drawings, gouaches, and paintings by Nattier, Lancret, Boucher, and Prud'hon in abundance, and busts of the Grand Dauphin and the duc d'Orléans by Coysevox now in the National Gallery in Washington. The former glory of Lord Hertford and Richard Wallace, Pepita's unanticipated inheritance, Seligmann's treasure—all dispersed to the four corners of the world's museums and private collections.

So much for the collection. As for the château, it was henceforth completely empty, as it had been over a century earlier, just after the Revolution. But it was not abandoned. On the contrary, the estate would become a special meeting place for Parisians and people passing through town. It was a place both inside and outside the city, to get away, to meditate, to fall in love, to celebrate. A place where people could get back in touch with themselves, back in touch with others, and also back in touch with a certain historical tradition and that refined French spirit the baronne d'Oberkirch once ascribed to the comte d'Artois.

Throughout the twentieth century, various public and private initiatives helped to sustain that spirit. First of all came the grounds, a destination for countless promenades, wonderfully enhanced by the planting of a rose garden. Festivities were held there—of which just one famous example will be described below—as well as political events, numerous art exhibitions, and *concours d'élégance* ... Bagatelle came alive.

The rose garden, planted on the site of the riding ring formerly installed for the imperial prince, hosts an annual contest for new varieties of rose.

> The Rose Garden is even more than a simple, if superb, display of roses—it is also a crucial factor of rivalry and research in the realm of beauty. Through contests of new varieties, this interesting institution has significantly increased the keen attraction

FACING PAGE
Current view of the head gardener's house.

PAGE 245
Eugène Atget, *Water Lilies*, gelatin silver print from glass negative, c. 1910 (Metropolitan Museum of Art, New York). Atget probably took this photo as part of a series at Bagatelle in 1910, recording a peaceful moment at the water-lily pond. Jean-Claude Nicolas Forestier, who created this pond when renovating the grounds at that time, was a friend of Claude Monet and an admirer of the artist's garden at Giverny.

PAGES 246–47
Jean-Claude Nicolas Forestier, *The Grounds at Bagatelle*, color print published in *Bagatelle et ses jardins*, 1910 (Bibliothèque Nationale de France). Director of woods and gardens for the western sector of Paris from 1898 onward, Forestier was behind the establishment of a rose garden at Bagatelle and the renovation of its grounds, showing great foresight by retaining their "Anglo-Chinois" appearance.

"Bagatelle. Those long hours in a garden, are perhaps the best things life will have given us."

Henry de Montherlant, *Le Figaro*, August 1, 1932

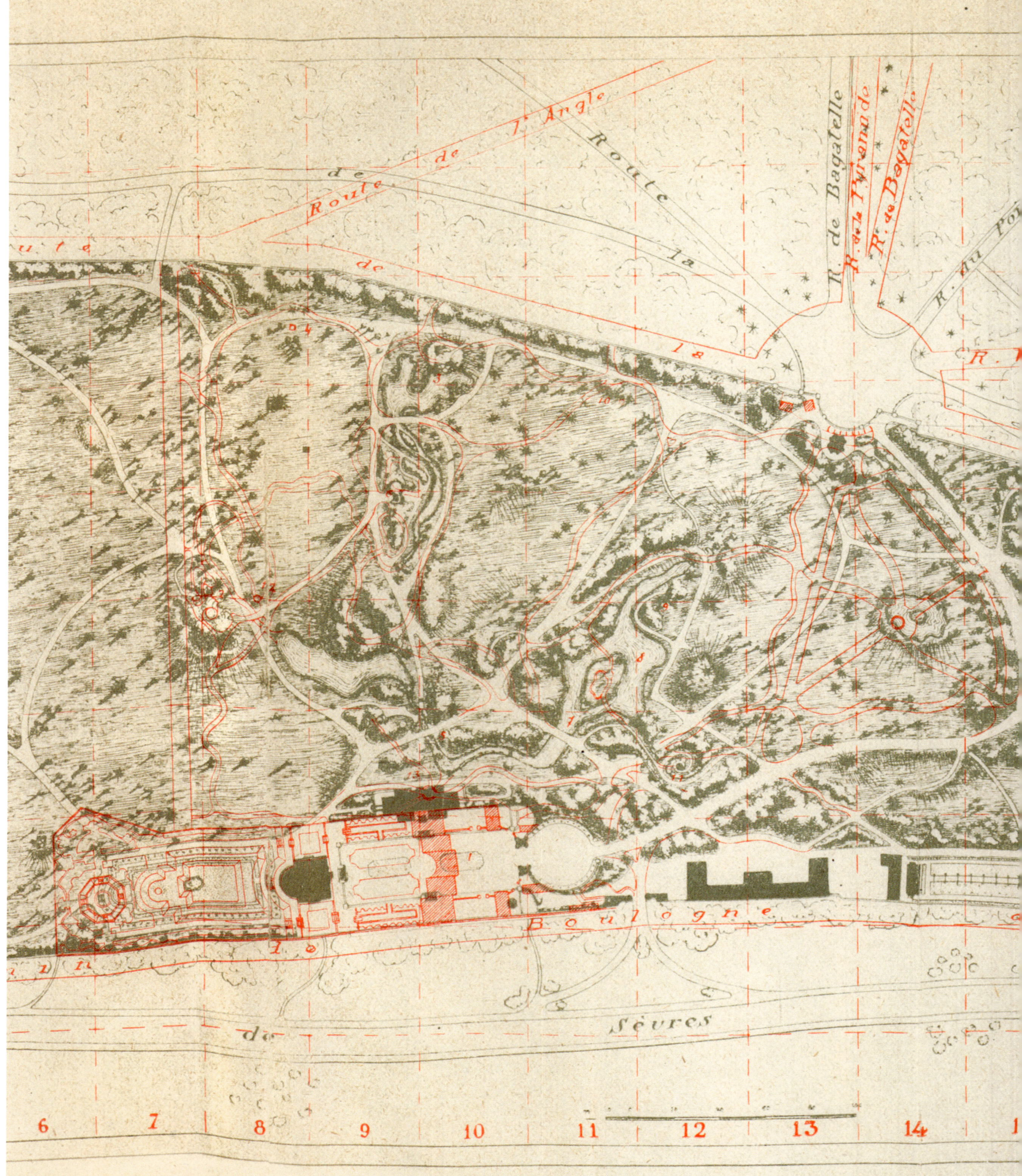

Route de l'Angle
Route de la
R. de Bagatelle
R. de la Pyramide
R. de Bagatelle
Boulogne
de
Sèvres
6
7
8
9
10
11
12
13
14

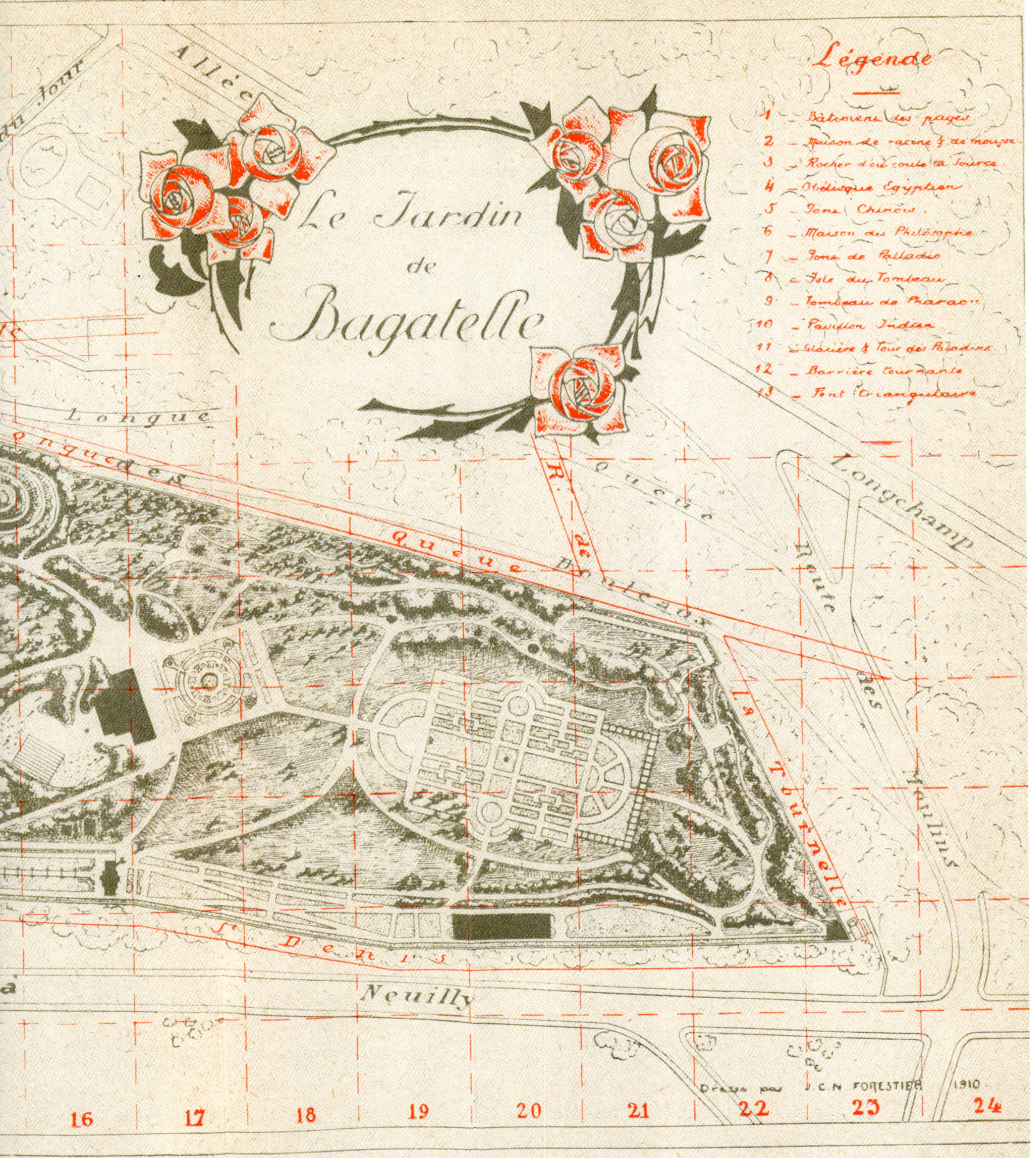
Le Jardin de Bagatelle
Légende
1 – Bâtiment des pages.
2 – Maison de racine & de mousse.
3 – Rocher d'où coule la Source.
4 – Obélisque Égyptien
5 – Pont Chinois.
6 – Maison du Philosophe
7 – Pont de Palladio
8 – Isle du Tombeau
9 – Tombeau de Pharaon
10 – Pavillon Indien
11 – Glacière & Tour des Paladins.
12 – Barrière tournante
13 – Pont triangulaire
Allée
Longue
Longchamp
Queue
Queue
Bouleaux
R. de
Route des Moulins
La Tournelle
St Denis
Neuilly
Dressé par J.C.N. FORESTIER 1910
16 17 18 19 20 21 22 23 24

29855

PAGES 248–49
Louise Deglane, *A Parisian Lady Strolling in the Rose Garden at Bagatelle*, autochrome (Société Française de Photographie). In 1907 Forestier came up with the idea of an international contest for new roses, bringing worldwide notoriety to Bagatelle's rose garden. The arbor, or Allée aux Arceaux, covered with climbing roses, remains a marvel even today.

PAGES 250–51
A photograph of the garden at Bagatelle by the Rol photo agency, 1913 (Bibliothèque Nationale de France). Forestier retained the orangery flowerbeds laid out in Hertford's day. They now lead to the rose garden, which replaced a riding ring used during the Second Empire, still overlooked by a little gazebo that served as a vantage point for Empress Eugénie, who monitored the riding lessons given to her son, the imperial prince.

RIGHT
Girl in a Straw Hat in the Rose Garden at Bagatelle, autochrome, c. 1920 (private collection). The autochrome process, marketed from 1907 onward, made color photography possible, becoming a favorite of lovers of gardens and flower shows.

"As soon as one crossed the front gate, one entered the Unknown, the Mysterious, the realm of Dreams.... There followed, slowly, a fantastic promenade along paths of silence, across lawns of silken grass, among roses that exhaled intoxicating fragrances. On occasion, there suddenly emerged from the shadow—in a brief glow sometimes pinkish, sometime bluish—a waterfall, a pond, or the strange outline of some rocky outcrop, like a huge ghost come to haunt the night."

Le Gaulois, July 18, 1909

"Monsieur Fabre-Luce came to fetch me at four thirty to go and have tea at the Château de Bagatelle. We went for a stroll in the beautiful gardens. We find there a well-heeled public, a very pleasing sight indeed."

Ferdinand Bac, *Livre-Journal*, April 17, 1921

> and profound esteem in which all visitors and admirers hold it. Messrs Gravereaux and Forestier, the organizers of this original contest, which began in 1906, have thus been able to awaken new curiosity and lively interest among the public in general and horticulturalists in particular.[190]

Jean-Claude Nicolas Forestier, who studied at the prestigious École Polytechnique before entering the École Nationale Forestière, was appointed director of woods and gardens for the western sector of Paris in 1898, and he pioneered not only the renovation of the grounds and the creation of a rose garden but also, more broadly, a vision of the future of Bagatelle. He researched the history of the estate and demonstrated remarkable farsightedness in preserving the "Anglo-Chinois" aspect of the grounds in opposition to prevailing fashion in the early twentieth century.[191]

When it comes to festive parties, we could hardly overlook the one given by the comtesse Greffulhe on July 17, 1909, which long impressed itself on people's memories. Not only was it mentioned by Marcel Proust (who modeled his character of the duchesse de Guermantes on the countess), but also an enthusiastic account was published the very next day in a major newspaper, *Le Gaulois.*

> The party at Bagatelle—It took place. You may be surprised, you may smile, but you would be wrong. It took place, and it was charming. All day long people hesitated. Would it rain, or would it not? Looking at their barometers—which also hesitated—elegant Parisian ladies first asked themselves whether or not they should go; then whether they should wear the pink outfit or a rain cloak; meanwhile, the organizers were also anxiously studying the sky.... Finally, after lengthy discussions, a decision was reached.... It was decided that the night would be warm and mild, and that some lamps would be lit there.... Thus before a dazzling assembly, in the most delightful and beautiful setting, we witnessed the most stirring show imaginable.
>
> In honor of the guests, Sleeping Beauty's woods came awake. As soon as one crossed the front gate, one entered the Unknown, the Mysterious, the realm of Dreams. Ahead were the deep woods, delicately lit by garlands of luminous spheres hanging from the branches, swaying beneath the leaves, which the dew adorned with gem-like finery, and which the mild night softly rocked. There followed, slowly, a fantastic promenade along paths of silence, across lawns of silken grass, among roses that exhaled intoxicating fragrances. On occasion, there suddenly emerged from the shadow—in a brief glow sometimes pinkish, sometime bluish—a waterfall, a pond, or the strange outline of some rocky outcrop, like a huge ghost come to haunt the night.

After having described the whole spectacle with delight, including a list of the most glamorous guests, the reporter concluded with an account of the fireworks. "It was inevitable, of course, that the evening end in a phantasmagoria—thus the night suddenly lit up with innumerable fantastic lights. The pond, the château, the orangery, and woods blazed with a dazzling glow, while from the lake there sprang cascades and palaces of fire as skeins of light crossed the sky like comets falling from heaven.... The comtesse Greffulhe is a decidedly generous fairy."[192]

PAGE 255
The main gate to the grounds of Bagatelle (detail).

FACING PAGE
Five O'clock Tea at Bagatelle, photograph, c. 1908 (private collection). Bagatelle was opened to the public following its purchase by the City of Paris in 1905. Among the first festivities held there in the early twentieth century, a party given by the comtesse Greffulhe on July 17, 1909, long remained in people's memories.

PAGES 258–59
Car Show at Longchamp Racetrack: Mademoiselle Raquel Meller with Hispano, Rol photo agency, 1928 (Bibliothèque Nationale de France). Automobiles and high fashion became inextricably associated with Bagatelle in the twentieth century. The grounds of the estate, along with the Longchamp racetrack and polo grounds, became the setting for annual car shows.

1910
BERNARD
B DE MONVEL

FACING PAGE
Bernard Boutet de Monvel, *Prince Léon Radziwill on the Polo Grounds at Bagatelle*, colored engraving, 1910 (private collection). Founded in 1891, the Polo Club de Paris was a private, exclusive club that rented grounds on the plain of Bagatelle from the Paris city council. The club's first president was the vicomte de la Rochefoucauld.

ABOVE
Pierre Mourgues, *Tea on the Polo Grounds at Bagatelle*, color print published in *L'Illustration*, 1926. An iconic high-society venue, the Polo Club at Bagatelle became an internationally famous institution over the years.

Proust should have written that article, but didn't. In frail health and at work on his magnum opus, *Remembrance of Things Past*, he turned down the invitation. Yet in his reply to the countess, the not-yet-famous author extolled the grounds at Bagatelle, which themselves contained "all the fragrances [he had] failed to harvest." His letter began with an apology:

> It is such a great joy for me—of which I am so unworthy, but by which I am so touched—that I fear you will misunderstand when I decline your invitation, that you will think I attach so much importance to what I am writing, when in fact I attach none. Not so long ago it was I who beseeched you concerning the publication of a very long article on yourself, which you consigned to a cruel fate. My admiration has not changed, it has thoroughly increased. Bagatelle is thoroughly you. You take such a uniquely graceful hold of the places you embrace that everything which previously existed there is forgotten.... Your gracefulness is imbued with the mysterious essence of the past, your gestures seem to scatter its ashes from some priceless urn. I know not whether I shall be in a condition on Saturday to get up for a few hours and go to Bagatelle. I have cancelled all my outings this year, one after another, and I was saving this one in order to experience, in a single blossom, all those fragrances I failed to gather. I hope and scarcely believe it—yet I would truly like to get there. And above all I would be so happy to get a glimpse of you, which I have not done for so many years."[193]

Bagatelle also hosted other gatherings, military and political, with different—though no less significant—stakes and priorities. In 1919, Paris troops returning from the front were assembled there, to the sound of patriotic verse and tunes like the "Chanson de Roland," the "Marche des Gardes du Roy," and the "Marche des Grenadiers." Some twenty years later, Bagatelle welcomed the British king, George VI, and his wife, Elizabeth. The former residence of the very anglophile comte d'Artois, once owned by two British subjects, thus hosted the monarch from across the Channel. The date was July 19, 1938. Times were troubled once again, as witnessed by the statement made by French prime minister Albert Lebrun. "More than ever, the perfect entente between two peoples, so fertile in every field, seems like a key element of security and concord, to the great benefit of peace and civilization."[194] His sentiments were echoed by George VI. "Despite the Channel separating us, with the passing of time our two countries have ineluctably joined their fates, and it is impossible to recall a time when our relationship was any closer."[195]

Between official ceremonies and displays, the British king and queen took the time to see a show of English art at the Louvre and to visit the hospital founded by Richard Wallace. Following an official parade, a magnificent dinner was held in the Hall of Mirrors at Versailles, followed by a concert of music by Lully in the Chapel Royal and a theatrical interlude in the Apollo Grove on the grounds of the château. The true moment of relaxation, however, came during a garden party at Bagatelle, which took up a whole afternoon. Five o'clock tea was followed by a ballet. The king was all smiles—the worries of the day were briefly forgotten.

After World War II, President Charles de Gaulle was welcomed by large crowds on the lawns of Bagatelle for his Labor Day speeches. In May 1974, it was the turn of the newly elected president, Valéry Giscard d'Estaing, to be fêted by a reception at Bagatelle. In 1992, Queen

FACING PAGE
The fashion model Capucine posing before a Delahaye automobile at the car show held in June 1951.

PARVA SED APTA

Elizabeth II, accompanied by Prince Philip, visited the Rose Garden and a show of sculptures by Henry Moore on the grounds.

Indeed, Bagatelle began hosting exhibitions in the early twentieth century. In 1908 there was a retrospective exhibition of portraits of famous men and women (1830–1900), another of "portraits of women under the three French republics" in 1909,[196] and yet another on "fashion through the centuries" in 1911. Such shows continued up to the last major exhibition, devoted to the works of famous designers Claude and François-Xavier Lalanne, in 1998.

Other displays of beauty graced the twentieth century. Fashion shows were held at Bagatelle in the 1930s, while the annual "classic car show" took place on the grounds from 1988 to 2000.

Bagatelle belongs to all. Everyone can experience it, can foster their own vision and memory of it, whether in tune with their own times or not. Yet no one is better placed to talk about Bagatelle than the people who take care of it. In 1956, Robert Joffet, head curator of parks and gardens for the City of Paris, wrote the forward to a book titled *Bagatelle et ses Jardins*. Before describing the floral gardens in detail, he presented his view of the estate and its history to "A Lady Friend of Bagatelle."

> The charming estate you are about to enter, Madame, belongs to women. Originally furnished by women, it was later transformed to receive them. When the youthful prince [comte d'Artois] wanted to win over a lady, he would take her in a fast carriage through the woods up to the country house, where she would arrive intoxicated by the air and the sweet words.
>
> She would cross a semicircle ringed by six statues, five of them female—silence, mystery, love, passion, and folly—the sixth being Hercules in all his dazzling attributes, indicating just how visitors to the estate would spend their time.
>
> The carriage would halt in front of the little château, that temple of love. The young lady would get down, helped by the prince who could then appreciate the delicate charm of the pressure of a hand, the lowering of eyelids, the bending of a head, the enigma of a smile—all indispensable preliminaries to the ultimate act of total abandonment.
>
> Revolution drove the prince away, but the ladies remained. During the Directorate, Bagatelle was turned into a park for popular entertainment, becoming the favorite promenade of fashionable youths known as Incroyables and Merveilleuses, as well as a meeting place for the prettiest, most elegant women of Paris.
>
> You will be happy here, Madame, if you love flowers. Like you, they live, breathe, grow, and blossom; like you, perhaps, they seek lovers. Thus, in order to help you appreciate the charm of Bagatelle all the more, I have tried to follow my predecessor, Monsieur Forestier, in extending and amplifying the floral harmonies that light up the grounds over the various seasons of the year.... For you, Madame, the grounds of Bagatelle—free and whimsical in design, adorable to behold, and welcoming to pretty ladies—will remain a place for promenades, created with the same fond wish that so inspired our eighteenth-century forebears: the wish to please.[197]

FACING PAGE
The ballet company known as Le Grand Ballet du Marquis de Cuevas rehearses *La Corrida* and *Gisèle* for a performance at Bagatelle, June 6, 1957.

PAGES 266–67
Georges Barbier, *The Party Ends with an Illumination at the Château de Bagatelle*, color print published in *L'Illustration*, 1924. Barbier, a fashion illustrator as well as a theatrical set designer, here offers a Roaring Twenties interpretation of a traditional French *fête galante*, imaginatively blending Bagatelle with the Trianon at Versailles.

PAGE 269
First edition of Chateaubriand's memoirs of the duc de Berry (collection of the author) placed on a table by Denizot for Bagatelle (Galerie Aveline, Paris).

PAGE 270
Detail of a door panel from one of the boudoirs flanking the grand salon.

PAGE 274–75
View of the courtyard façade.

Notes

Chapter 1

1 Marianne Gilbert, *Le Bois de Boulogne* (Paris: La Bibliothèque des Arts, 1958), 22–23.
2 Roger Baschet, *Mademoiselle Dervieux, fille d'Opéra* (Paris: Flammarion, 1943), 68, quoting Cardinal Fleury's *Mémoirs*. On Mademoiselle Dervieux, see chapter 3.
3 Charles Philippe Albert, duc de Luynes, *Mémoires du duc de Luynes sur la cour de Louis XV* (Paris: Firmin Didot, 1864), XVI: 161.
4 Edmond-Jean-François Barbier, *Chronique de la Régence et du règne de Louis XV* (Paris: Classiques Garnier 2020), I: 166.
5 Louis XV was twenty-eight at the time. Argenson dates his affair with Madame de Mailly to March 1736. "The king wished to fondle a woman other than the queen, so Madame de Mailly was settled on him."
6 Marquis d'Argenson, *Journal et mémoires du marquis d'Argenson* (Paris: Veuve Jules Renouard, 1859), II: 11.
7 Ibid., II: 12.
8 L. de Quellern, *Le Château de Bagatelle* (Paris: Charles Foulard, n.d. [c. 1909]), 14.
9 Marquis d'Argenson, *Journal*, V: 254.
10 Charles Gailly de Taurines, *Aventuriers et femmes de Qualité* (Paris: Hachette, 1907), 189.
11 Duc de Luynes, *Mémoires*, XVI: 161.
12 Two copies of the manuscript exist, one in the Bibliothèque de l'Arsenal, Paris, and the other in the archives of the city of Nancy. The excerpts here are taken from Gaston Duchesne, *Le Château de Bagatelle 1715–1908* (Paris: Jean Schemit, 1909), 45 ff.
13 Duc de Luynes, *Mémoires*, XVI: 161.
14 Duchesne, *Le Château de Bagatelle*, 50.
15 Quoted in Duc de Luynes, *Mémoires*, XVI: 165.
16 Quoted in Duchesne, *Le Château de Bagatelle*, 117–118.

Chapter 2

17 Louis Petit de Bachaumont *et al.*, *Mémoires Secrets pour servir à l'histoire de la République des Lettres en France* (London: J. Adamson, 1784), X: 259.
18 Marie Antoinette, *Correspondance 1770–1793*, ed. Évelyne Lever (Paris: Tallandier, 2005), 211.
19 Ibid., 191.
20 Ibid., 198.
21 Ibid., 213. The term "liaison" employed by Mercy-Argenteau does not mean a sex affair in the modern sense, but a close—and publicly visible—friendship. Recent biographies of Marie Antoinette tend to confirm that her only real lover was comte Axel de Fersen, later in the 1780s. See also Évelyn Lever, *Le grand amour de Marie Antoinette—Lettres secrètes de la reine et du comte de Fersen* (Paris: Tallandier, 2020). On the other hand, the rumor of a real affair between Marie Antoinette and Artois was regularly fueled at the time by scurrilous satires, such as *Les amours de Charlot et Toinette*, an almost pornographic piece of street verse.
22 Ibid., p. 214. The empress referred to "printed papers" to avoid directly mentioning her source, Mercy-Argenteau.
23 Ibid., 215.
24 Georges Bordonove, *Les Rois qui ont fait la France. Charles X, dernier roi de France et de Navarre* (Paris: Pygmalion, 1990), 21.
25 John Hardman, *Marie Antoinette, The Making of a French Queen* (New Haven: Yale University Press, 2019), 26 ff.
26 *Mémoires de Madame Campan, première femme de chambre de Marie Antoinette* (Paris: Mercure de France, 1988), 67.
27 Quoted in Pierre de Ségur, *Marie Antoinette* (Paris: Calmann Lévy, 1916), 9.
28 On the comte de Vaudreil, see Benedetta Craveri, *Les Derniers Libertins* (Paris: Flammarion, 2016), 347–398.
29 *Mémoires autographes de Monsieur le Prince de Montbarey* [*sic*] (Paris: Alexis Eymery et Rousseau, 1826) II: 221–222.
30 *Mémoires de la comtesse de Boigne* (Paris: Mercure de France, 1971), 42.
31 Colin B. Bailey, *Patriotic Taste—Collecting Modern Art in Pre-revolutionary Paris* (New Haven: Yale University Press, 2002), 163–206.
32 Francis Haskell, *Rediscoveries in Art* (Oxford: Phaidon, 1976), 25–35.
33 Élisabeth Vigée-Lebrun, *Memoirs*, trans. Sian Evans (Bloomington: Indiana University Press, 1989), 35.
34 Geneviève Haroche-Bouzinac, *Louise-Élisabeth Vigée-Lebrun—Histoire d'un regard* (Paris: Flammarion, 2011) and Bailey, *Patriotic Taste*.
35 Vigée-Lebrun, *Memoirs*, 347.
36 Ibid., 347.
37 Ibid., 348.
38 In a letter to Maria Theresa dated February 28, 1776, Mercy-Argenteau described a visit to Bagatelle by Marie Antoinette. See *Correspondance secrète entre Marie-Thérèse et le Cte Mercy-Argenteau* (Paris: Firmin Didot, 1874), II: 426.
39 Letter from Mercy-Argenteau to Maria Theresa dated November 19, 1777. *Correspondance secrète*, III: 135–136.

Chapter 3

40 Claude Godart d'Aucourt, *Thermidore, ou mon histoire et celle de ma maîtresse*, quoted in Claire Ollagnier, *Petites maisons. Du refuge libertin au pavillon d'habitation* (Paris: Editions Mardaga, 2016), 36, which discusses this phenomenon.
41 "I hope his majesty will be pleased by the simplicity and nobility of the architecture." Letter from Gabriel to the marquis de Marigny, June 1752. Quoted in Jean-Marie Pérouse de Montclos, *Ange Jacques Gabriel, l'héritier d'une dynastie d'architecte* (Paris: Éditions du Patrimoine, 2012), 35.
42 Jean-Marie Pérouse de Montclos, *Histoire de l'architecture française de la Renaissance à la Révolution* (Paris: Editions Menges/Editions du Patrimoine, 1995/2003), 394.
43 Luc-Vincent Thiery, *Guide des amateurs et des étrangers voyageurs à Paris* (Paris: Hardouin et Gattey, 1788), 28.
44 On Bélanger, see Jean Stern, *À l'ombre de Sophie Arnould, François-Joseph Bélanger, architecte des Menus Plaisirs, premier architecte du comte d'Artois* (Paris: Plon, 1930), and Alexia Lebeurre and Claire Ollagnier (eds), *François-Joseph Bélanger, Artiste Architecte* (Paris: Picard, 2021).
45 John Harris, "Sir William Chambers and His Parisian Album," *Architectural History* 6 (1963), 55 and 79.
46 John Harris and Michel Snodin (eds), *Sir William Chambers—Architect to George III* (New Haven: Yale University Press/Courtault Institute of Art, 1997), 84.
47 These two drawings are held at the Victoria and Albert Museum, and are illustrated in *Sir William Chambers, Catalogues of Architectural Drawings in the Victoria & Albert Museum*, ed. Michael Snodin (London: V&A Publications, 1996), 159–160 and 173–177.
48 The chest has unfortunately vanished, but a drawing survives. Charlotte Vignon and Christian Baulez (eds), *Pierre Gouthière, Virtuoso Gilder at the French Court* (New York: The Frick Collection, 2016), 298–299.
49 *Vues pittoresques: Plans et descriptions des principaux jardins anglais qui sont en France* (no publisher, c. 1780–85).
50 Mary L. Myers, *French Architectural and Ornament Drawings of the Eighteenth Century*, catalog of the exhibition (New York: Metropolitan Museum of Art, 1992), 18 (no. 12) and xxv (color plate 12). See also Peter Fuhrung, *François-Joseph Bélanger, 1744–1818*, *Cahier du Dessin Français* 15 (Galerie de Bayser, 2006), notably examples 9, 10, 29, and 31.

51 On the history of grotesque decoration and the influence of the Vatican Loggias in the eighteenth century, see Alexandra Zamperini, *Les Grotesques* (Paris: Citadelles Mazenot, 2007); Anne Gilet (ed), *Giovani Volpato–Les Loges de Raphaël et la Galerie du Palais Farnèse*, catalog of the exhibition (Tours: Musée des Beaux-Arts de Tours/Silvana Editoriale, 2007); and Nicole Dacos, *La Découverte de la Domus Aurea et la Formation des Grotesques à la Renaissance* (London: The Warburg Institute, 1969), notably 107–113 on the role of Giovanni da Udine in the execution of Raphael's Loggias.

52 Vitruvius, *The Ten Books of Architecture*, trans. Morris Hicky Morgan (Cambridge, Mass.: Harvard University Press, 1914), book VI, ch. V, para. 3.

53 C. H. Watelet, *Encyclopédie, ou dictionnaire raisonné des sciences, des arts et des métiers* (Paris, 1757).

54 *Vues pittoresques: Plans et descriptions des principaux jardins anglais qui sont en France* (no publisher, c. 1780–85).

55 "Mémoire des ouvrages de sculpture faits par Lhuillier, sculpteur rue du faubourg Saint-Denis, sous les ordres de M. Bellanger, premier architecte de Monseigneur," Archives Nationales, R1 82.

56 Christian Baulez, "Les bronziers Gouthière, Thomire et Rémond," in Catherine Gendre (ed), *Louis Simon Boizot 1743–1809, sculpteur du roi et directeur de l'atelier de sculpture à la manufacture de Sèvres* (Paris: Somogy, 2001), reprinted in *Versailles, deux siècles d'histoire de l'art, Études et chroniques de Christian Baulez* (Versailles: Société des Amis de Versailles, 2007), 403–420.

57 "Mémoire d'horlogerie pour Monseigneur le comte d'Artois qui comprend deux pendules faites par ordre de M. de Ste-Foy, l'une placée à St Germain en 1780 et l'autre dans le salon de Bagatelle au commencement de 1781, plus les 1500 l. pour l'entretien des pendules et horloges pendant l'année 1782, par Lepaute, horloger du Roy et de Monseigneur le comte d'Artois," Archives Nationales, R1 260.

58 "Mémoire de l'horlogerie fournie, pendant les années 1777–1780, par Lepaute, horloger du Roi," Archives Nationales, R1 260. Confiscated during the Revolution, this clock was dispatched to the Ministry of Finances on 29 Ventôse Year IV (March 19, 1796), and described as follows: "A clock by Lepaute, topped by a globe of the earth supported by clouds, accompanied by two children, one of whom represents day, holding in his hand a pointer that indicates the time, and the other partly wrapped in a nocturnal cloak, representing night, the garland set in front of the truncated column of white marble rising to the hinge, hiding the square by which the clock must be wound, width 5 inches 6 lines, height 14 inches," Archives Nationales, 02 433.

59 "Mémoire d'ouvrages de bronzes ciselés et dorures mates fournis pour Monseigneur le comte d'Artois à Bagatelle, sous la conduite de M. Jubault son Garde meuble général par Rémond, doreur, rue des Petits Champs, Saint-Martin, mars 1780," Archives Nationales, R1 264.

60 Pierre Gouthière, Charlotte Vignon and Christian Baulez (eds), *Pierre Gouthière, Virtuoso Gilder at the French Court* (New York: The Frick Collection, 2016), 264–275. See also 276–279 for an illustration of Bélanger's design for a fireplace for the duchesse de Mazarin, drawn when it was installed in the château de Ferrières; a copy of this fireplace was placed in the dining room of Bagatelle in the nineteenth century.

61 These chests of drawers were identified by Alexandre Pradère.

62 Ulrich Leben, "An Armchair and Folding Screen for the comte d'Artois at Bagatelle," *Furniture History: The Journal of the Furniture History Society* 43 (2007), 127–141.

63 Drouot sale, March 6, 2000, lot 89.

64 *Décors, mobilier et objets d'art du Louvre–de Louis XIV à Marie-Antoinette* (Paris: Louvre/Somogy, 2014), 434–435. See also Michel Beurdeley, *Georges Jacob et Son Temps* (Saint-Rémy-en-l'eau: Monelle Hayot, 2002), 20–21.

65 The armchair was sold at Christie's London on June 23, 1999, for £386,500. The bedroom furniture was sold at Artcurial Paris on July 22, 2020, for 1,174,500 €.

66 Bachaumont, *Mémoires Secrets* XV: 168 (May 26, 1780).

67 A drawing attributed to Bélanger and acquired by the Amis du Château de Bagatelle in the 1980s seems to be a sketch of it.

68 Baron Paul Thiébault, *Mémoires du Genéral Thiébault* (Paris: Plon, 1906), I: 156.

69 Bachaumont, *Mémoires Secrets*, XV: 167 (May 26, 1780).

70 Tony-Henri-Auguste, vicomte de Reiset, *Marie-Caroline, duchesse de Berry, 1816–1830* (Paris: Goupil & Co. 1906), 157. Reiset added, "The betraying mirrors have vanished, along with the libertine paintings decorating the little house of the prince, whose youthful years were taken up with dissolute pastimes that only his age could excuse."

71 Jean-Marie Pérouse de Montclos, *Étienne Louis Boullée, 1728–1799–De l'architecture classique à l'architecture révolutionnaire* (Paris: Arts et Métiers Graphiques, 1969), 74–76 and 109. Quoted by Charlotte Vignon, *Turkish Taste at the Court of Marie-Antoinette*, unpublished lecture given at the Frick Collection, July 27, 2011. A mirror-lined boudoir was also installed by Pierre Élisabeth de Fontanieu at the Garde-Meuble de la Couronne in 1772; see Guillaume Faroult, *L'Amour Peintre, l'imagerie érotique au XVIIIe siècle* (Paris: Cohen & Cohen, 2020), 170–172.

72 Dufort de Cheverny, *Mémoires sur les règnes de Louis XV et Louis XVI et sur la Révolution 1732–1802* (Paris: Plon Nourrit, 1886), I: 305.

73 Since November 22, 1775, Boullée had served as intendant of works for the comte d'Artois, whose household included a superintendant, intendant, first architect, and so on. In 1777 Bélanger became the count's first architect–not intendant–yet his arrival seems to have provoked Boullée's resignation. See Pérouse de Monclos, *Étienne Louis Boullée*, 109.

74 Antoine Caillot, *Mémoires pouvant servir à l'histoire des moeurs et usages des français* (Paris: Dauvin, 1827 [Geneva: Slatkine Reprints]), II: 99–101. Quoted (in French) in Diana Cheng, *The History of the Boudoir in the Eighteenth Century* (PhD thesis, McGill University, 2011).

75 Jacques Silvestre de Sacy, *Alexandre Théodore Brongniart, 1739-1813, sa vie, son œuvre* (Paris: Plon, 1940), 36-38.

76 Roger Baschet, *Mademoiselle Dervieux, fille d'Opéra* (Paris: Flammarion, 1943), 97 ff.

Chapter 4

77 David Watkins, *The English Vision: The Picturesque in Architecture, Landscape and Garden Design* (London: John Murry, 1982), VIII.

78 Thomas Blaikie, *Diary of a Scotch Gardener at the French Court at the End of the Eighteenth Century* (London: Routledge, 1931; Cambridge University Press, 2012), 166–167. The spelling and grammar are obviously Blaikie's.

79 "make-believe and surprise also played a vital role in the Picturesque."

80 A "ha-ha," in addition to onomatopoeia for laughter, is a ditch with an inner wall below ground level, forming a boundary to a park without interrupting the view, hence the "surprise" of experiencing the boundless landscape.

81 On the history of English gardens and their influence on France, see Watkins, *The English Vision*, chapters 1–4 and 7 ("English Influence Abroad"); Nikolaus Pevsner, "The Genesis of the Picturesque," *Studies in Art, Architecture and Design* (London: Thames & Hudson, 1968), 79–101; and Monique Mosser, "La Perfection du Jardin Anglo-Chinois," in Martine Constans (ed), *Bagatelle dans ses jardins* (Paris: Action artistique de la Ville de Paris, 1997), 135–177.

82 Sir William Temple, *Upon the Gardens of Epicurus, with Other XVIIth Century Garden Essays* (London: Chatto & Windus, 1908), 53–54.

83 Quoted in Pevsner, "The Genesis of the Picturesque," 83.

84 Mosser, "La Perfection," quoting Jurgis Baltrušaitis, *Aberrations, Quatre essais sur la légende des formes–Jardins et Pays d'Illusion* (Paris: Olivier Perrin, 1957).

85 Quoted in Watkins, *The English Vision*, 68.

86 Watkins, *The English Vision*, 162.

87 Patricia Taylor, *Thomas Blaikie, the 'Capability' Brown of France, 1751–1838* (Tuckwell Press, 2001), chapters 7–9. Taylor's title is slightly misleading.

88 Stern, *À l'ombre de Sophie Arnould*, I: 30.

89 Bachaumont, *Mémoires secrets*, XV: 167 (May 26, 1780).

90 See the legend on the plan published by Le Rouge in 1784.

91 Thiery, *Guide des amateurs*, 26–27.

92 These gouaches, probably commissioned by the comte d'Artois, were known only from engravings published in *Vues pittoresques de France* in the late 1780s. They recently resurfaced on the art market; I would like to thank the Galerie Aaron for its kind permission to reproduce them.

[93] The quote states that M. de Dillon played "the conceited character, M. de Besenval the financier, M. d'Adhémar the fool, M. de Coigny the noble father, and M. de Vaudreuil the mentor. Dazincourt and Dugazon were summoned to direct rehearsals, and soon everyone had learned their role as best they could." Duchesne, *Le Château de Bagatelle*, 143.
[94] Blaikie, *Diary of a Scotch Gardener*, 167.
[95] Duchesne, *Le Château de Bagatelle*, 147.
[96] Blaikie, *Diary of a Scotch Gardener*, 182.
[97] Ibid., 182–183.
[98] Ibid., 183.
[99] Henriette Louise von Waldner, baronne d'Oberkirch, *Mémoires de la baronne d'Oberkirch* (Paris: Charpentier, 1853), 283.
[100] Lebeurre and Ollagnier, *François-Joseph Bélanger*, 56–58.
[101] *Mémoires de Madame Campan* (Paris: Mercure de France, 1988), 112, 267–268, 346.
[102] Blaikie, *Diary of a Scotch Gardener*, 223.
[103] Ibid., 224.
[104] Ibid., 229–230.
[105] Alste Oncken, *Friedrich Gilly 1772–1800* (Berlin: Mann Verlag, 1936/1981), 83–84. David Watkin and Tilman Mellinghoff, *German Architecture and the Neoclassical Ideal* 1740–1840 (London: Thames & Hudson, 1987), 70–71.
[106] Friedrich Gilly, "A description of the Villa of Bagatelle, near Paris," in Gilly, *Essays on Architecture 1796–1799*, trans. David Britt (Los Angeles: The Getty Center for History of Art and the Humanities, 1994), 139 ff. See also the last chapter, on the architectural heritage of Bagatelle.
[107] Kurt W. Foster, *Schinkel, A Meander Through his Life and Work* (Basel: Birkhaüser Verlag 2018), 290–291.
[108] Gilly, *Essays on Architecture*.
[109] Ibid., 147.

Chapter 5

[110] François René, vicomte de Chateaubriand, *Memoirs, Letters, and Authentic Details Relating to the Life and Death of H.R.H. Monseigneur Charles Ferdinand d'Artois, Duc de Berry*, trans. anon. (London, 1821), 52–154. [The translator would like to thank Valerie C. Stenner of Special Collections, Morris Library, University of Delaware, for sourcing this nineteenth-century translation, slightly modified here.] The same anecdote is found in Édouard Hocquart, *Le Duc de Berry, ou Vertus et Belles Actions d'un Bourbon* (Paris: Didot, 1820), 29–30.
[111] Handwritten letter addressed to Sophie Arnould held at the Bibliothèque Nationale de France.
[112] Pierre-François-Léonard Fontaine, *Journal 1799–1853* (Paris: École Nationale Supérieure des Beaux-Arts/Institut Français d'Architecture, 1987), 265–267.
[113] Christophe de Michel du Roc, called Duroc, duc de Frioul, nicknamed "Napoleon's shadow," was Napoleon's grand marshal of the palace. "Service du Grand Maréchal du Palais," Archives Nationales, O[2] 225, 235.
[114] Archives Nationales O[2] 560. The residence in question was the former hôtel Marbeuf, bought by the Bonapartes in 1803 and sold in 1810. In 1887 it was demolished and rebuilt in a Louis-XV revival style by Frédéric Pillet-Will, director of the Bank of France. Today it serves as the residence of the Japanese ambassador to France.
[115] On hunting practices during the Empire and Restoration, see Charles-Éloi Vial, *Le Grand Veneur de Napoléon Ier à Charles X* (Paris: École des chartes, 2016), especially 99 and 617–618.
[116] *Mercure de France*, December 1, 1810, 39–40. The reporter was mistaken about the date and placement of the motto, *Parva sed apta*.
[117] *Enfance impériale, le Roi de Rome, fils de Napoléon*, catalog of the exhibition (Fontainebleau, 2011), 67.
[118] Fontaine, *Journal*, I: 510–511. See also Edouard Driault, *Napoléon Architecte* (Paris: PUF, n.d.), 145–146.
[119] Fontaine, *Journal*, I: 350.
[120] On this subject, see Laetitia de Witt, *L'Aiglon* (Paris: Taillandier, 2020), 57.
[121] Louis Constant Wairy, called Constant, *Mémoires de Constant, premier valet de chambre de l'Empereur* (Paris: Ladvocat, 1830), IV: 331–334. The comtesse de Montesquiou-Fezensac, nicknamed "Maman Quiou," was the king of Rome's governess.
[122] Thanks to artist Jacques Louis David, Fontaine met Joséphine, and then Napoleon, in 1799. He became the government's architect during the Consulate and, later, first architect to the emperor. He kept his job during the Bourbon Restoration, becoming municipal architect for Paris, architect to the king, and architect to the duc d'Orléans.
[123] Fontaine, *Journal*, I: 436.
[124] Philip Mansel, *Paris Between Empires* (London: John Murray, 2001), 194.
[125] See the biography by Laure Hillerin, *La Duchesse de Berry: L'Oiseau rebelle des Bourbons* (Paris: Flammarion, 2016).
[126] Vial, *Le Grand Veneur*, 197 and 453.
[127] *Journal des Débats* (July 14, 1814), 2.
[128] *Mémoires de la Duchesse de Gontaut* (Paris: Plon-Nourrit, 1909), 142.
[129] *Journal de l'Empire* (April 2, 1815), quoted in Vial, *Le Grand Veneur*, 166.
[130] *Journal des Débats* (January 27, 1817), 5.
[131] The painting is included in the duc de Berry's inventory of paintings at Bagatelle in 1820, and then in the duchess's inventory of paintings at the Tuileries Palace in 1822. See Féréol Bonnemaison, *Galerie de son Altesse Royale Madame la Duchesse de Berry* (Paris: J. Didot, 1822), I: 192. The presence of the stuffed eagle at Bagatelle is attested in the same document.
[132] Reiset, *Marie-Caroline*, 51.
[133] Ibid., 111. The wet-nurse was one Sophie de Witte, wife of a Monsieur Bayart, a notary at Armentières and a certified royalist.
[134] Ibid., 159.
[135] Fontaine, *Journal*, II: 828.
[136] The anecdote is contemporary with the assassination of the duc d'Enghien, hence dates from 1804, when Vigée-Lebrun and the royal family were both in London. Vigée-Lebrun, *Memoirs*, 256.
[137] Étienne Breton and Pascal Zuber, *Boilly, Le Peintre de la Société Parisienne de Louis XVI à Louis-Philippe* (Paris: Arthena, 2019), I: 79 and 426. The main works are described in Charles-Paul Landon's review of the Salon.
[138] On the duchesse de Berry's artistic tastes, see Béatrice de Brimont, "La duchesse de Berry. Un amateur illustre sous la Restauration," *L'Estampille, L'Objet d'Art* 255 (February 1992), as well as Brimont's essay in Hildegard Kremer (ed), *Marie Caroline de Berry–Naples, Paris, Graz, itinéraire d'une princess romantique* (Paris: Somogy, 2002), 160.
[139] See Vial, *Le Grand Veneur*, 453–454.
[140] They were replaced in 1835 due to their poor condition. See the next chapter.
[141] Archives Nationales, *Fonds du château de Rosny, Duc et Duchesse de Berry, Château de Bagatelle* (1814-1824), 371AP/10.
[142] Sosthène de La Rochefoucauld, *Mémoires*, XIV: 287, quoted in Vial, *Le Grand Veneur*, 546.
[143] *Translator's note:* In the chaos of the collapse of the Second Empire, Henri was briefly offered the throne as a compromise solution, but he notoriously insisted that the nation abandon its blue-white-and-red flag and return instead to the monarchical fleur-de-lis flag, at which point the compromise deal fell apart.
[144] Fontaine, *Journal*, II: 918.
[145] Thomas Raikes, *A Portion of the Journal Kept by Thomas Raikes, Esq. from 1831 to 1847* (London: Longman, Brown, Green, Longmans & Roberts, 1858), I: 146.

Chapter 6

[146] George Augustus Frederick assumed the regency in 1811, later reigning himself as George IV from 1820 to 1830.
[147] On the lives of the 4th Marquess and Richard Wallace, see David Mallet, *The Greatest Collector, Lord Hertford and the Founding of the Wallace Collection* (London: MacMillan 1979); Peter Howard, *Sir Richard Wallace, the English Millionaire of Paris, and the Hertford British Hospital* (Grimsay Press, 2009); and Suzanne Higgott, *The Most Fortunate Man of His Day–Sir Richard Wallace* (London: The Wallace Collection, 2018). In French, Lydie Perreau published a semi-fictional novel, *La Fortune de Richard Wallace* (Paris: Lattès, 2009).
[148] She not only inherited from the duke, "Old Q," but also from her other adoptive father, George Selwyn.
[149] Lord Henry was the illegitimate son of Mie-Mie and Casimir Montrond, one of Talleyrand's agents.

[150] Francis Hibbert, *George IV: Regent and King* (Allen Lane, 1973), 85 and 263.
[151] Bernard Falk, *"Old Q's" Daughter: The History of a Strange Family* (London: Hutchinson, 1951), 164.
[152] First called Hertford House, then St. Dunstan, the residence became the St. Dunstan Institute for the Blind until it was finally bought by Barbara Hutton, who demolished it to build Winfield House, currently the residence of U.S. ambassadors in London.
[153] Mansel, *Paris Between Empires*, 333, quoting Cavour.
[154] Ibid., 366, quoting the dandy Roger de Beauvoir.
[155] Comtesse Le Hon, dubbed "the golden-haired ambassadress," was the wife of the Belgian ambassador and the mistress of the duc d'Orléans.
[156] On Marie d'Orléans's tastes, see Anne Dion-Tennebaum (ed), *Marie d'Orléans, princesse et artiste romantique, 1813–1839* (Paris: Somogy, 2008).
[157] Pauline Prévost-Marcilhacy, *Les Rothschild, bâtisseurs et mécènes* (Paris: Flammarion 1995), 45–48 and 55–65.
[158] On this subject, see *La Collection La Caze*, the catalog of the Louvre exhibition of the same name (Paris: Louvre/Hazan, 2007), notably the essays by: Guillaume Farout on knowledge of old masters in France in 1830–70 (p. 47); Carole Blumenfeld on the pioneers of the rediscovery of the eighteenth century (p. 85); and Jo Hedly on Hertford's tastes and purchases (p. 97).
[159] On the nineteenth-century prices of works by Watteau, Greuze, Boucher, and Fragonard, notably the prices paid by Hertford, see Gerald Reitlinger, *The Economics of Taste: The Rise and Fall of Picture Prices*, 1760–1960 (London: Barrie & Rockliff, 1961), 184–186.
[160] Edmond and Jules de Goncourt, *L'Art du XVIIIe siècle* (Paris: Charpentier, 1881). The first volume opens with the line, "Watteau was the great poet of the eighteenth century."
[161] The Wallace Collection also holds the masterpieces by Boucher. On the 1860 exhibition, see Farout's essay in *La Collection La Caze*, 107. On the nineteenth-century "rediscovery" of eighteenth-century painting, see also Haskell, *Rediscoveries in Art*, especially chapter 3 on "The Two Temptations." Finally, see the proceedings of the symposium organized by the Wallace Collection and the Louvre during the *Collection La Caze* show: *Delicious Decadence: The Rediscovery of French Eighteenth-century Painting in the Nineteeth Century*, ed. Guillaume Faroult, Monica Preti, and Christoph Vogtherr (Farnham: Ashgate Publishing, 2014), chapters 2 and 7.
[162] "Les grandes collections étrangères," *Gazette des Beaux-Arts* (January 1, 1873).
[163] On the Rothschilds's collections and comparison of their purchases to Hertford's, see Pauline Prévost-Marcilhacy, *Les Rothschilds, Une Dynastie de Mécènes en France* (Paris: Louvre/Somogy, 2016), especially III: 326 ff.
[164] Raikes, *A Portion of the Journal*, 399. As per British custom, Hertford was called by his courtesy title, Lord Yarmouth, having not yet inherited the title of marquess from his father, who was still alive.
[165] On architectural modifications and interior decoration of that period, see Alice Thomine, "La période anglaise," in Constans, *Bagatelle dans ses jardins*, 111–130.
[166] *Le Moniteur des Architectes* (1873), 168.
[167] This desk can be identified in Bagatelle by a 1902 photograph reproduced in the *Bulletin de la Société historique d'Auteuil et de Passy* (April 1909), 314. After the sale of Bagatelle, it can be seen in a photograph of the Grande Galerie at 2 rue Laffitte, published in A. F. Morris, *The Connoisseur* (1910), XXVII: 231.
[168] Alexandre Ananoff, *François Boucher. Catalogue raisonné de l'œuvre* (Paris: La Bibliothèque des arts, 1976), 273, n. 154.
[169] Christophe Pincemaille, "L'impératrice Eugénie et Marie Antoinette autour de l'exposition rétrospective des souvenirs de la reine au Petit Trianon en 1867," *Versalia* 6 (2003), 124–134. The list of twenty-three items lent by Hertford can be found in note 20.
[170] Edmond and Jules de Goncourt, *Pages from the Goncourt Journal*, ed. and trans. Robert Baldick (Harmondsworth: Penguin, 1984), 153–154. "Brother Seymour" was Hertford's half-brother, Lord Henry Seymour-Conway.
[171] Hertford's illness prompted the following comment from the Goncourts: "Ah, a great avenger of wealth and great poisoner of millions is death. The Englishman with ten million a year, Hertford, who has a rotten bladder and cannot buy a new one, despite all his money, said glumly to Claudin: 'I've seen all the doctors, even summoned them from England: my only remedy is [the cemetery of] Père Lachaise.'"
[172] Henri Rochefort, *Les Aventures de ma vie* (Paris: Dupont, 1896–1898), I: 114–115.
[173] Madame Carette, née Bouvet, *Souvenirs intimes de la cour des Tuileries* (Paris: Paul Ollendorff, 1891), III: 226–227.
[174] Horace de Viel Castel, *Les Mémoires du comte Horace de Viel Castel* (Paris: Chez Tous les Libraires, 1883), III: 310, (October 23, 1856). Viel Castel was a curator at the Louvre from late 1852 to 1863.
[175] Benedetta Craveri, *La Contessa* (Paris: Flammarion, 2021), 106. See also *La comtesse de Castiglione par elle-même* (Paris: Musée d'Orsay, 1999).
[176] Viel Castel, *Les Mémoires*, IV: 173 (September 14, 1857).
[177] Lady Elizabeth Eastlake, *Letters and Journals of Lady Eastlake* (London: John Murray, 1895), II: 154–155 (October 21, 1860).
[178] Viel Castel, *Mémoires*, I: 54 (February 20, 1851).
[179] *Le Journal des Goncourts*, X: 41 (November 9, 1871). It was the Goncourts who nicknamed Sabatier "La Présidente." Her salon played a major role in the art scene during the Second Empire; Bernard Falk has compared it to the Bloomsbury group in London.
[180] Wallace also helped to finance reconstruction of the headquarters of the Légion d'Honneur, which had been destroyed during the events of the Paris Commune.
[181] On various aspects of Wallace's art patronage in the United Kingdom and France, see chapter 7, "Taking Art to the Public," in Higgott, *The Most Fortunate Man*, 273–317.
[182] Henry James, *The Complete Writings of Henry James on Art* (Cambridge: Cambridge University Press 2016), 7.
[183] In the 1870s Wallace bought two works by Heilbuth directly from the artist, *Excavations in Rome* and *The Cardinal*. See *The Wallace Collection's Pictures* (London: Unicorn Publishing Group), 201.
[184] *L'Univers illustré* (August 2, 1890).

Chapter 7

[185] Quoted in Higgott, *The Most Fortunate Man*, 340.
[186] The *Times*, July 22, 1890, quoted in Peter Hughes, *The Founders of the Wallace Collection* (London: Trustees of the Wallace Collection, 1981), 54.
[187] Germain Seligmann, *Merchants of Art, 1880–1960: Eighty Years of Professional Collecting* (New York: Appleton-Century-Crofts, 1961), 92–103 (99 and 101 for the passages quoted here).
[188] Ibid., 100–101.
[189] Ibid., 100–101.
[190] Quellern, *Le Château de Bagatelle*, 85.
[191] Monique Mosser, "Notes brèves à propos de Forestier," in Constans, *Bagatelle dans ses jardins*, 204–205.
[192] *Le Gaulois*, July 18, 1909, article on the first page of the society notes ("Bloc Note Parisien"), signed "Tout-Paris."
[193] Laure Hillerin, *La comtesse Greffulhe: L'ombre des Guermantes* (Paris: Flammarion, 2014).
[194] *La visite en France des souverains britanniques* (Paris: Éditions d'Histoire et d'Art/Plon, 1938), 4.
[195] Ibid., 5.
[196] These shows were organized by the Société Nationale des Beaux-Arts and were accompanied by illustrated catalogs.
[197] Foreword to André Leroy, *Bagatelle et ses Jardins* (Paris: Baillère et Fils, 1956). J. C. N. Forestier, mentioned in the final paragraph, created the Rose Garden and in the 1920s published a book with the same title—*Bagatelle et ses jardins* (Paris: Librairie agricole de la Maison rustique)—but with different content.

PARVA S

APTA

Selected Bibliography

Among the numerous sources used, particularly memoirs, testimonies, and reference books, these were particularly useful and are a good source for those who wish to go deeper into the subject.

Alcouffe, Daniel, Colin Bailey, and Claude Arnaud. *La Folie d'Artois*. Paris: Antiquaires à Paris, 1988.

Bailey, Colin B. *Patriotic Taste: Collecting Modern Art in Pre-Revolutionary Paris*. New Haven and London: Yale University Press, 2002.

Constans, Martin, ed. *Bagatelle dans ses jardins*. Paris: Action artistique de la Ville de Paris, 1997.

Craveri, Benedetta. *Les Derniers Libertins*. Paris: Flammarion, 2016.

Duchesne, Henri-Gaston. *Le Château de Bagatelle*. Paris: Jean Schemit, 1909.

Éloy, Sophie, and Guillaume Faroult, eds. *La Collection La Caze. Chefs-d'œuvre des peintures des XVIIe et XVIIIe siècles du musée du Louvre*. Paris: Musée du Louvre Éditions / Hazan, 2007. Exhibition catalog.

Falk, Bernard. *"Old Q's" Daughter: The History of a Strange Family*. London: Hutchinson, 1951.

Gilet, Anne, ed. *Giovani Volpato—Les Loges de Raphaël et la galerie du palais Farnèse*. Tours: Musée des Beaux-Arts de Tours / Silvana Editoriale, 2007. Exhibition catalog.

Hardman, John. *Marie Antoinette, The Making of a French Queen*. New Haven and London: Yale University Press, 2019.

Haroche-Bouzinac, Geneviève. *Louise Élisabeth Vigée-Lebrun—Histoire d'un regard*. Paris: Flammarion, 2011.

Harris, John, and Michel Snodin, eds. *Sir William Chambers: Architect to George III*. New Haven and London: Yale University Press / Courtauld Institute of Art, 1997.

Haskell, Francis. *Rediscoveries in Art*. Oxford: Phaidon, 1976.

Higgott, Suzanne. *The Most Fortunate Man of His Day—Sir Richard Wallace*. London: The Wallace Collection, 2018.

Hillerin, Laure. *La Duchesse de Berry—L'Oiseau rebelle des Bourbons*. Paris: Flammarion, 2016.

Lebeurre, Alexia, and Claire Ollagnier, eds. *François-Joseph Bélanger: Artiste architecte*. Paris: Picard, 2021.

Mallet, David. *The Greatest Collector: Lord Hertford and the Founding of the Wallace Collection*. London: MacMillan, 1979.

Mansel, Philip. *Paris Between Empires*. London: John Murray, 2001.

Marie-Caroline de Berry. *Naples, Paris, Graz—Itinéraire d'une princesse romantique*. Paris: Somogy, 2002.

Ollagnier, Claire. *Petites maisons. Du refuge libertin au pavillon d'babitation*. Brussels, Mardaga, 2016.

Prévost-Marcilhacy, Pauline. *Les Rothschild, bâtisseurs et mécènes*. Paris, Flammarion, 1995.

De Reiset, Tony-Henri-Auguste. *Marie-Caroline, duchesse de Berry, 1816–1830*. Paris: Goupil & Co. 1906.

Seligmann, Germain. *Merchants of Art, 1880–1960: Eighty Years of Professional Collecting*. New York: Appleton-Century-Crofts, 1961.

Stern, Jean. *À l'ombre de Sophie Arnould, François-Joseph Bélanger, architecte des Menus Plaisirs, premier architecte du comte d'Artois*. Paris: Plon, 1930.

Taylor, Patricia. *Thomas Blaikie: The 'Capability' Brown of France, 1751–1838*. East Linton: Tuckwell Press, 2001.

Vial, Charles-Éloi. *Le Grand Veneur de Napoléon Ier à Charles X*. Paris: École des chartes, 2016.

Vignon, Charlotte, and Christian Baulez, eds. *Pierre Gouthière, Virtuoso Gilder at the French Court*. New York: The Frick Collection, 2016.

Watkins, David. *The English Vision: The Picturesque in Architecture, Landscape and Garden Design*. London: John Murry, 1982.

Sources of Quotations

PAGE 7
Henry James, *The Spoils of Poynton* (Boston and New York : Houghton, Mifflin and Company, 1897), 12.

PAGE 12
Charles Gailly de Taurines, *Aventuriers et femmes de Qualité* (Paris: Hachette, 1907), 175.

Henry James, *William Wetmore Story and His Friends* (London: Thames & Hudson, 1903), I: 125.

PAGE 20
Bonamy Dobrée, ed., *The Letters of Philip Dormer Stanhope, 4th Earl of Chesterfield* (New York: Ams Press, 1932), III: 977.

PAGE 24
Marquis d'Argenson, *Journal et mémoires du marquis d'Argenson* (Paris: Veuve Jules Renouard, 1859), II: 137.

PAGE 30
Voltaire, "Impromptu à Mademoiselle de Charolais," in *Œuvres complètes de Voltaire: Stances, odes, contes en vers, satires, poésies mêlées* (Paris: J. Esneaux, 1823), 344.

PAGE 37
Marquis d'Argenson, *Journal et mémoires du marquis d'Argenson* (Paris: Veuve Jules Renouard, 1859), V: 254.

PAGE 42
Marie Antoinette, *Correspondance 1770–1793*, ed. Évelyne Lever (Paris: Tallandier, 2005), 211.

PAGE 51
Mémoires de Madame Campan (Paris: Mercure de France, 1988), 145.

PAGE 55
Quoted in Pierre de Ségur, *Marie-Antoinette* (Paris: Calmann-Lévy, 1916), 9.

PAGE 63
Correspondance secrète entre Marie-Thérèse et le Comte de Mercy-Argenteau (Paris: Firmin-Didot, 1874), III: 135–136.

PAGE 70
Friedrich Gilly, "A description of the Villa of Bagatelle, near Paris," in *Essays on Architecture 1796–1799*, trans. David Britt (Los Angeles, CA: The Getty Center for History of Art and the Humanities, 1994), 139 ff.

PAGE 97
"Bagatelle," in *Vues pittoresques: Plans et descriptions des principaux jardins anglais qui sont en France* (n.d. [c. 1780–85]), n.p.

PAGE 108
Tony-Henri-Auguste, vicomte de Reiset, *Marie-Caroline, duchesse de Berry, 1816–1830* (Paris: Goupil & Co. 1906), 157.

PAGE 116
Quoted in Henri-Gaston Duchesne, *Le Château de Bagatelle* (Paris: Jean Schemit, 1909), 285.

PAGE 123
Quoted in Janine Barrier, *William Chambers: Une architecture empreinte de culture française* (Paris: Presses de l'Université Paris-Sorbonne, 2010), 211.

PAGE 130
Louis Petit de Bachaumont, *Mémoires Secrets pour servir à l'histoire de la République des Lettres en France* (London: J. Adamson, 1786), XXIV: 49.

PAGE 141
Henriette Louise von Waldner, baronne d'Oberkirch, *Mémoires de la baronne d'Oberkirch* (Paris: Mercure de France, 1989), 467–468.

PAGE 148
Tony-Henri-Auguste, vicomte de Reiset, *Marie-Caroline, duchesse de Berry, 1816–1830* (Paris: Goupil & Co. 1906), 56.

PAGE 166
Journal des Débats Politiques et Littéraires, August 25, 1814, 3.

PAGE 184
William Bürger, "Les Collections Particulières," in *Paris Guide par les principaux écrivains et artistes de la France* (Paris: Librairie Internationale, 1867), II: 537 ff.

Henry James, *The Complete Writings of Henry James on Art* (Cambridge, MA: Cambridge University Press 2016), 58.

PAGE 194
"Les grandes collections étrangères," *Gazette des Beaux-Arts*, January 1, 1873, 70.

PAGE 218
Madame Carette, née Bouvet, *Souvenirs intimes de la cour des Tuileries* (Paris: Paul Ollendorff, 1891), III: 226–227.

PAGE 234
Marcel Proust, quoted in Laure Hillerin, *La comtesse Greffulhe. L'ombre des Guermantes* (Paris: Flammarion, 2014), 380–381.

PAGE 244
Henry de Montherlant, "Bagatelle," *Le Figaro*, August 1, 1932, 1.

PAGE 254
"Bloc-Notes Parisien. La Soirée de Bagatelle," *Le Gaulois*, July 18, 1909, 1.

PAGE 256
Ferdinand Bac, *Livre-Journal 1921* (Paris: Éditions Claire Paulhan, 2022), 192.

Index

Page numbers in *italic* refer to captions.

Photographic Credits

t: top, b: bottom, l: left, r: right

All photographs in this book were taken by Bruno Ehrs except those on the following pages:

p. 9: © Clément Prats; p. 21: © Suzanne Tise-Isoré; p. 22: © PVDE/Bridgeman Images; p. 25: © RMN-Grand Palais (Château de Versailles)/Gérard Blot; p. 26: © Château de Versailles, Dist. RMN-Grand Palais/Christophe Fouin; pp. 28–29: © The Wallace Collection, London, Dist. RMN-Grand Palais/The Trustees of the Wallace Collection; p. 31: © RMN-Grand Palais (Château de Versailles)/Gérard Blot/Christian Jean; p. 32: © Private collection; p. 35: © BnF; p. 36: © Private collection/photo © David Bordes; p. 39: © RMN-Grand Palais (Château de Versailles)/El Meliani; p. 44: © Agefotostock/Photo12/J.D. Dallet; p. 47: © Château de Versailles, Dist. RMN-Grand Palais/Christophe Fouin; p. 49: © Fondation Mansart/photo © David Bordes; p. 50: © RMN-Grand Palais (musée du Louvre)/Thierry Le Mage; p. 53: © Östergötlands Museum; photo: Jim Löfgren; p. 54: © RMN-Grand Palais (Château de Versailles)/Gérard Blot; p. 57: © RMN-Grand Palais/Agence Bulloz; p. 58: © The National Gallery, London, Dist. RMN-Grand Palais/National Gallery Photographic Department; p. 61: © CC0 Paris Musées/Musée Carnavalet – Histoire de Paris; p. 62: © CC0 Paris Musées/Musée Carnavalet – Histoire de Paris; p. 66: © BnF; p. 67: © Fondation Mansart/photo © David Bordes; pp. 68–69: © All rights reserved; p. 72: © Elger Esser; p. 74: © Courtesy of Ministero della Cultura-Gallerie Estensi, Biblioteca Estense Universitaria; p. 75t: © Photo Scala, Florence/V&A Images/Victoria and Albert Museum, London; p. 75b: © Photo Scala, Florence/V&A Images/Victoria and Albert Museum, London; p. 77: © akg-images; pp. 78–79: © Ville de Paris/Bibliothèque historique, réserve D 134; p. 80: © akg-images/CDA/Guillot; pp. 82–83: © BnF; p. 88: © The Metropolitan Museum of Art, Dist. RMN-Grand Palais/image of the MMA; p. 89: © The Metropolitan Museum of Art, Dist. RMN-Grand Palais/image of the MMA; p. 90l: © The Metropolitan Museum of Art, Dist. RMN-Grand Palais/image of the MMA; p. 90r: © The Metropolitan Museum of Art, Dist. RMN-Grand Palais/image of the MMA; p. 91l: © The Metropolitan Museum of Art, Dist. RMN-Grand Palais/image of the MMA; p. 91r: © The Metropolitan Museum of Art, Dist. RMN-Grand Palais/image of the MMA; pp. 92–93: © The Metropolitan Museum of Art, Dist. RMN-Grand Palais/image of the MMA; p. 96: © Nicolas Cattelain; p. 99: © Nicolas Cattelain; p. 100: © All rights reserved; p. 101: © All rights reserved; p. 102: © All rights reserved; p. 103: © All rights reserved; p. 104: © Nicolas Cattelain; p. 107t: © BnF; p. 107b: © CC0 Paris Musées/Musée Carnavalet – Histoire de Paris; p. 108: © Nicolas Cattelain; p. 109: © Galerie Talabardon & Gautier, Paris/Guillaume Benoit; p. 110: © Waddesdon Image Library, Mike Fear; p. 112: © Wallace Collection, London, UK/Bridgeman Images; p. 113: © Galerie Talabardon & Gautier, Paris/Guillaume Benoit; pp. 114–15: © The Metropolitan Museum of Art, Dist. RMN-Grand Palais/image of the MMA; p. 117: © Suzanne Tise-Isoré; p. 118: © Bernd. H Dams and Andrew Zega, Architectural Watercolors; p. 121: © All rights reserved; p. 122: © BnF; pp. 124–25: © All rights reserved; p. 127: © BnF; pp. 128–29: © All rights reserved; p. 131: © BnF; pp. 132–33: © Drawing Matter; p. 134: © The Metropolitan Museum of Art, Dist. RMN-Grand Palais/images of the MMA; pp. 138–39: © Musée Carnavalet/Roger Viollet; p. 140: © Suzanne Tise-Isoré; p. 143: © Wallace Collection, London, UK/Bridgeman Images; p. 144: © RMN-Grand Palais (PBA, Lille)/Stéphane Maréchalle; p. 150: © CC0 Paris Musées/Musée Carnavalet – Histoire de Paris; p. 153: © Private collection; pp. 154–55: © CC0 Paris Musées/Musée Carnavalet – Histoire de Paris; p. 156: © Bridgeman Images; p. 159: © RMN-Grand Palais (musée du Louvre)/Michel Urtado; pp. 160–61: © CC0 Paris Musées/Musée Carnavalet – Histoire de Paris; p. 163: © Akg-images/Album; p. 164: © RMN-Grand Palais (Château de Fontainebleau)/Adrien Didierjean; p. 167: © RMN-Grand Palais (Château de Versailles)/Franck Raux; pp. 168–69: © National Trust Photographic Library/Bridgeman Images; p. 170: © RMN-Grand Palais (Château de Versailles)/Franck Raux; pp. 172–73: © His Majesty King Charles III, 2022/Bridgeman Images; p. 175: © photo Irwin Leullier/Musée de Picardie, Amiens; pp. 178–79: © CC0 Paris Musées/Musée Carnavalet – Histoire de Paris; p. 186: © Wallace Collection, London, UK/Bridgeman Images; pp. 188–89: © All rights reserved; p. 191: © Wallace Collection, London, UK/Bridgeman Images; p. 192: © Art Digital Studio © Sotheby's; p. 195: © The Wallace Collection, London, Dist. RMN-Grand Palais/The Trustees of the Wallace Collection; p. 197: © CC0 Paris Musées/Musée Carnavalet – Histoire de Paris; pp. 198–99: © CC0 Paris Musées/Musée Carnavalet – Histoire de Paris; p. 201: © CC0 Paris Musées/Musée Carnavalet – Histoire de Paris; pp. 202–3: © Clément Prats; pp. 204–5: © CC0 Paris Musées/Musée Carnavalet – Histoire de Paris; p. 209: © Suzanne Tise-Isoré; p. 210: © Fondation Mansart/photo © David Bordes; p. 211: © Nicolas Cattelain; pp. 212–13: © Fondation Mansart/photo © David Bordes; p. 215: © Fondation Mansart/photo © David Bordes; p. 219: © CC0 Paris Musées/Musée Carnavalet – Histoire de Paris; pp. 220–21: © CC0 Paris Musées/Musée Carnavalet – Histoire de Paris; pp. 222–23: © CC0 Paris Musées/Musée Carnavalet – Histoire de Paris; p. 224: © Library of Congress; p. 229: © National Portrait Gallery, London; pp. 232–33: © Galerie ARY JAN; p. 236: © Tallandier/Bridgeman Images; p. 240: © Suzanne Tise-Isoré; p. 241: © Christie's Images/Bridgeman Images; p. 242: © Suzanne Tise-Isoré; p. 245: © The Metropolitan Museum of Art, Dist. RMN-Grand Palais/image of the MMA; pp. 246–47: © BnF; pp. 248–49: © Collection Société française de photographie (coll. SFP); pp. 250–51: © BnF; pp. 252–53: © The Holbarn Archive/Bridgeman Images; p. 256: © Maurice-Louis Branger/Roger-Viollet; pp. 258–59 : © BnF; p. 260: © Bernard Boutet de Monvel/Jacques Pépion; p. 261: © All rights reserved; p. 263: © AGIP/Bridgeman Images; p. 264: © Jack Garofalo/ParisMatch/Scoop; pp. 266–67: © Photo12/L'Illustration.

Every effort has been made to identify the photographers and copyright holders of the images reproduced in this book. Any error or omissions referred to the Publishers will be corrected in subsequent printings.